FÉB
1996

Secret Squadrons of the Eighth

Secret Squadrons of the Eighth

specialtypress

Previous page:
Groundcrew prepare to load leaflet bombs into a B-17 at Cheddington, as two aircrew members look on.
Imperial War Museum (IWM) OWIL 29629

Maps by Mike Keep

Published by Speciality Press, Publishers and Wholesalers
P.O. Box 338
123 North Second Street
Stillwater, MN 55082 U.S.A.
In Minn 612-430-2210
Toll-free 800-888-9653

Printed in England
90 91 92 93 94 5 4 3 2 1
ISBN 0-933424-43-4

First published in the United Kingdom by Ian Allan Ltd. Book trade distribution by Voyageur press, Inc.

Speciality Press books are also available at discounts for quantities for educational, fundraising, premium, or sales-promotion use. For details contact the marketing manager. Please write or call for a free catalog of aviation publications.

CONTENTS

ACKNOWLEDGEMENTS

There are so many people without whose invaluable assistance this book could not have been written. In particular there are those members of the Cheddington (STN 113) Association, who served with units of the United States 8th Air Force (US 8th AF) during World War 2. It is, however, impossible for me to express my gratitude to each and every one individually. I therefore hope that they will forgive me.

During the many years of research that have culminated in the publication of this book, a number of units and institutions have been contacted or visited. In America they include the USAF Historical Research Center, Maxwell AFB, Alabama; the Inspection & Flight Safety Center, Norton AFB, California; the National Archives & Record Center; and the American Battle Monuments Commission, Washington DC. In England, the Air Historical Branch of the MOD and the Public Record Office, Kew; the Royal Signals & Radar Establishment, Malvern; and both the Imperial War Museum, Lambeth, and the RAF Museum, Hendon. I am indebted to the staff involved who assisted with my many requests for help and information.

A number of private individuals also contributed in more ways than they could possibly know: 'Willy' Donald kept my spirits up when the postman failed to arrive, and fellow 'Bud' drinker Steve Pigott, due to his criticism, gave me the determination to continue. Likewise so did Simon Waite, but in his case it was praise that kept me going. Ann-Marie Mitchell moved the commas and my sister Marie Harris exchanged the 'dones' for 'dids'.

Last but not least, if it had not been for the discomfort my wife Shirley and two children Peter and Marie suffered from the continuous buzz of my printer, then this book would never have been completed.

To all of you I say 'thank you'.

Pat Carty
England 1989

'What will become of this little section of England that has been our life for the last year or two? Will the runways and hardstands lay abandoned and untouched in mute tribute to the men who worked, lived and sweated out the planes during the years of war and restriction? What will become of the dogs once fed so well around the mess halls — the legion of station mascots? Will they walk through deserted kitchens wondering where the chow lines and their GI pals have gone? What impression have we Americans made in our frequent contacts with the English people who have been our neighbours, and companions, during these long monotonous war-weary years? Probably, these questions which probe into the future will not be answered for many years.'

American GI, Cheddington 1943

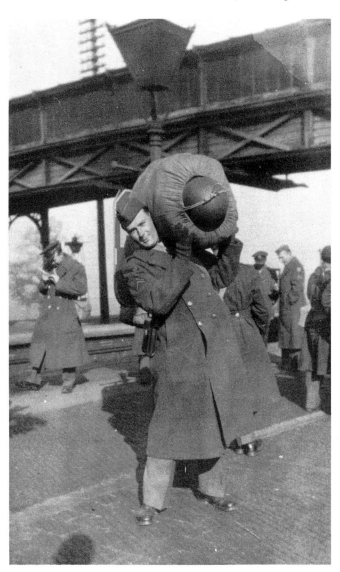

Right:
For the many American servicemen stationed at the nearby base, Cheddington railway station spelled journey's end after the arduous Atlantic crossing and wearying train ride from Liverpool Docks. Here men from the 1077th Signal Company arrive at Cheddington in June 1943. *B. Downs/113 Association*

I
THE HOME

Cheddington

Set in a triangle of countryside bounded by the tranquil villages of Long Marston, Cheddington and Marsworth, is an area of farmland reminiscent of the kind of setting seen in a John Constable painting. However, this is not what it turned out to be, for some 40 years ago this area became home to units of the United States Army Air Force (USAAF) whose missions were some of the best kept secrets of World War 2.

This area, 30 miles northwest of London and shared by the Home Counties of Buckinghamshire and Hertfordshire, had for many years been a quiet spot in the English countryside. Events in other parts of the country, however, were far from quiet. In response to the increasing threat of war — on 26 May 1939 — and as a result of the RAF's expansion plan — an 'Aerodrome Board' was formed by the Air Ministry. The Board members were instructed to seek sites for the building of airfields with the requirement that they be at least three to five miles apart and at least 50ft above sea level (ASL). This was to eliminate the risk of flooding, but the sites could be no more than 650ft ASL due to the problems this would engender from mist and fog. When such a site was found, and if it were free from obstructions, it would be marked off on an Ordnance Survey map within a 1,000yd circle. This circle would then be inspected for any minor obstructions and the proposed runways 'walked out'. Finally, a geological map (if one was available) was used to study the structure of the subsoil.

When two Long Marston farmers, and Arthur Reeve the tenant farmer of Church Farm, Marsworth, found out that a Mr Phipps from the 'Board' would be touring their area looking to requisition such land, they had no worries — or so they thought! What a shock however, when, soon after the visit and its ensuing meetings, they found out that their land, with two large hills to the northeast, Dunstable Downs to the southeast, and Marsworth Church to the southwest, had been one of 4,000 inspected sites and that it was now required! Arthur Reeve, who had farmed the area for many years, like his parents before him, not only had a shock, but could not believe his eyes when, within a few days of the visit, he received a letter instructing him not to plough his soil any more. If what he read in the letter was correct, and he forfeited his land, it would mean he would stand to lose his farmhouse; and if he lost that, he would lose his livelihood. For a man with a wife and young family, the future indeed looked bleak!

The area in question was soon requisitioned, trees removed and the surface levelled by gangs of workmen who had been

Left:
Church Farm, Marsworth in 1940. Arthur Reeve who farmed Church Farm had all his land requisitioned to enable Cheddington airfield to be built.

hired by a local government contractor, B. Sunley Ltd. However, progress was slow, so in June 1941 the Government brought in the well known construction firm of George Wimpey to take over the contract and finish the earth moving, cutting-out and laying of the runways, and erection of the main buildings. For the electrical installations, two firms — Malcome & Allen and Crompton Parkinson — were used. This left just the living sites to be constructed by G. Walker & Slater and Lansdown's. To improve the bricklaying time, an automatic bricklayer was used and put to work on the control tower. The bricklayer consisted of a box structure into which bricks and mortar were placed. This removed the need to line up each row. This 'quick' bricklaying method was of little benefit for after the brick walls had reached 3ft high, they were out of true by 3in. As the control tower was designed to be some 30ft in height, it would have been out of true by 30in on completion! This of course was not acceptable, so the whole construction was pulled down and rebuilt by hand, the finished article being a Type 13079/41 control tower.

The Royal Air Force

When all building work had been completed and the new airfield named 'Cheddington' after the nearest railway station, the Royal Air Force took command. As it had already been decided by the Air Ministry that the airfield was to be used as a bomber training airfield, and because the building of the runways on the nearby airfield at Wing in Buckinghamshire had not been concluded, it was agreed to move the Headquarters of No 26 Operational Training Unit (OTU), which was due to use Wing, into Cheddington. The date selected was 9 March 1942. On 15 March, 121 officers and other ranks of the OTU Servicing Squadron followed, and made preparations for the arrival of their aircraft. This did not take long as four Avro Ansons arrived on 22 March, followed the next day by the first of the unit's Vickers Wellington bombers. The first flight out was made on the 26th, when an Anson left conveying an instructor on liaison duties.

Within a month the number of aircraft assigned to the OTU was 17 Wellingtons and six Ansons. One of the Ansons, Mk I DJ124, had the distinction of being the unit's first aircraft to be damaged when it was involved in a ground accident on 3 April. Accidents, however, went hand-in-hand with training, as No 2 Squadron from RAF Sawbridgeworth could verify. Soon after it had set up a temporary camp at Cheddington on 27 April for Exercise 'Sapper', Curtiss Tomahawk Mk I, AH934 XV-O, flown by Plt Off Vaughan, damaged a wing. The purpose of the squadron exercise was for three Tomahawk aircraft to perform artillery reconnaissance (ARTY/R), tactical reconnaissance (TAC/R) and message dropping sorties in support of British Army units. The squadron must have taken a liking to Cheddington, as it returned for

Below:
Cheddington — General arrangement.

Above:
Marsworth village in September 1980. Shown are some of the areas used as living sites by the USAAF. Bucks Herald

Left:
In 1975 the northern section of Cheddington airfield was used by a unit of the American CIA, but those events — Operation 'Nine Alpha' — are another secret from another squadron. Post Echo

Below:
Cheddington airfield main gate and technical site — 1981. *113 Association*

Right:
Vickers Wellington BX LR132 of No 26 OTU which was stationed at Cheddington for the summer months of 1942. For most of the war the Wellington was the mainstay of No 26 OTU.
IWM HU1976

Below:
After eight months of operating the Curtiss Tomahawk, No 2 Squadron RAF converted to the North American Mustang I in April 1942. *IWM CH7058*

Exercise 'Sledgehammer' the following November with its Mustang Is.

The month of May brought bad news when the first aircraft loss was reported on the 31st. Wellington Mk IC DV707 EU-D was reported 'missing in action' (MIA), following the historic 1,000-bomber raid to Cologne. August was also a bad month, as three other Wellingtons were also struck off charge. On the 5th, X9675 caught fire and the crew had to abandon it over Burton Coggles near Grantham. On the 12th, DV868 EU-E, whilst landing one side of the flarepath, retracted the undercarriage to go round again. Air speed could not be maintained, and she stalled and burned out in the crash that followed. There were no injuries to the crew, however. This was not the case when, on the 30th, DV825 EU-U also burned out. She took off at 15.45hrs for circuits and landings, but lost speed, bounced, then swung round and stalled trying to clear the hill to the south of Cheddington airfield. The pilot, Sgt McDougall, and one of the gunners, Sgt Hendricksen, both died from burns despite being pulled from the flaming wreckage by Gordon Miller and his cowman Dan Millins of Manor Farm, Marsworth. These two rescuers received the British Empire Medal from the King for their brave actions.

The Mighty Eighth

When the construction of RAF Wing had been accomplished, it could not have been a day too soon for the men of the OTU to move in, and away from the hills and obstructions that were to be found around Cheddington airfield. Reports were soon submitted claiming that the airfield was unsuitable for RAF training purposes. Four days later, on 7 September 1942, the empty airfield was handed over to the United States 8th Army Air Force (8th AF). The intention was for it to become an administration satellite for nearby Bovingdon. The Americans during this time were deficient in the number of airfields available to meet their requirements, and wasted no time in accepting the airfield — not for administrative use, but as a base for their fast-growing air armada.

The period from March 1942, whilst the airfield at Cheddington had been experiencing growing pains, was also a time of great change for many units of the 8th AF. Far across the wide Atlantic in America, the 44th Bomb Group had been struggling to form itself into a fighting unit. The Group had been activated and trained at Barksdale Field, Louisiana, and were almost fully

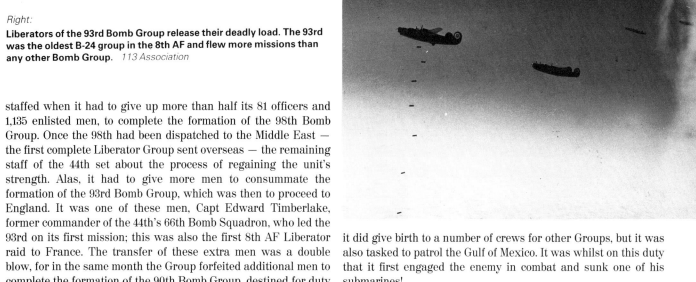

Right:

Liberators of the 93rd Bomb Group release their deadly load. The 93rd was the oldest B-24 group in the 8th AF and flew more missions than any other Bomb Group. *113 Association*

staffed when it had to give up more than half its 81 officers and 1,135 enlisted men, to complete the formation of the 98th Bomb Group. Once the 98th had been dispatched to the Middle East — the first complete Liberator Group sent overseas — the remaining staff of the 44th set about the process of regaining the unit's strength. Alas, it had to give more men to consummate the formation of the 93rd Bomb Group, which was then to proceed to England. It was one of these men, Capt Edward Timberlake, former commander of the 44th's 66th Bomb Squadron, who led the 93rd on its first mission; this was also the first 8th AF Liberator raid to France. The transfer of these extra men was a double blow, for in the same month the Group forfeited additional men to complete the formation of the 90th Bomb Group, destined for duty in Australia. It was a task that almost made the unit's staff officers 'throw in the towel'. All hope was not abandoned in the 44th, however, as the 8th AF 'Selective Service' machinery was functioning at full speed and during April more replacements poured in from Induction Centres all over the United States. By May, the 44th had a full complement, but then had to give up more officers and men (10 trained crews) to fill gaps in a number of other bomb groups. There was a further blow, for it had also to send a crew on a secret mapping expedition into the cold of the Arctic, the concept being to make the ever-increasing airways from North America to Europe a safer route to travel. This task they accomplished and, was a result, many fliers now owe their gratitude to that intrepid crew.

Do not be deceived however, as the stay for the 44th at Barksdale was more than a rest period at a maternity home. True,

it did give birth to a number of crews for other Groups, but it was also tasked to patrol the Gulf of Mexico. It was whilst on this duty that it first engaged the enemy in combat and sunk one of his submarines!

The sweltering days of July 1942 came, and the 44th proceeded to Will Rogers Field, Oklahoma City, to continue training, but with more vigour as the unit had been informed to prepare for overseas duty within three months. War does not wait, for within 30 days it was on its way overseas. The ground echelon was transported by three trains to Fort Dix, New Jersey where there was a mad scramble to procure extra equipment. On 3 September the officers and men piled on to special trains for Jersey City, and from there were ferried up the Hudson River to Cunard Dock where the liner *Queen Mary* was waiting. She set sail the next afternoon in brilliant sunshine down the Hudson, and out by the Statue of Liberty. Up past Coney Island, until the shores of America passed out of view, then nosed her way out into the cold Atlantic. Five mornings later she sailed down the Irish Sea, with a view of the green fields of Ireland to starboard and the rolling

Below:

**Training Record
Prior to service in England with the Night Leaflet Squadron, Gunner Jake Sandoval spent many hours training at Yuma and March AFB in America.**

Left:
Luther Walck (right) and Terry Olean of the 282nd Medical Dispensary, pictured at the local inn sampling a 'half an' half'. The Americans found English beer 'weak and warm'. *L. Walck/113 Association*

hills of Scotland to port. She dropped anchor in the Clyde, her men disembarked, then boarded trains for their new English home at Cheddington.

Back in America, the air echelon of the 44th was fighting the 'Battle of Camp Grenier', to obtain as much equipment as possible. When the battle had been won and the intensive training programme completed, it too left the beloved homeland. The echelon made the difficult North Atlantic crossing not by sea, but in 27 of its trusty B-24D Liberators. The first nine crews, from the 66th Squadron, arrived at Cheddington on 1 October and, once reunited, the officers and men of the air and ground echelons set out to firmly establish Anglo-American relationships whilst off-duty. When on duty there was an intensive programme of conditioning for the new climate and the environment. The men soon learned to say 'three ha'pennies', 'chairs', 'you cahn't miss it' and many other quaint old English figures of speech that were new to their ears. These soon became part of their everyday vocabulary. The men were also initiated into the English joys of drinking non-intoxicating warm beer, and the difficult task of hardening a certain part of their anatomy for a new mode of transport — the bicycle. This required learning to ride, for them, on the 'wrong' side of the road!

The stay at Cheddington for the 44th was short, for in less than a month the unit, together with its equipment and all but one Liberator, set off for another new home — Shipdham in Norfolk. The reason for leaving Cheddington was that the airfield was again found to be too small and the runway not long enough or hard enough to take the pounding of heavy bombers day after day. This change of station for the 44th changed its whole future, for had it remained at Cheddington on the training task intended, it would not have suffered 153 aircraft missing in action, or endured the tragic loss of life that resulted.

Meanwhile, the resident Clerk of Works for the Air Ministry was informed about the airfield's problems and he in turn informed his area office. As a result it was agreed that the 8th AF would move out and that extra construction would take place to enlarge the living, technical and recreation sites. On 26 October, with the exception of three officers and six enlisted men who remained on a 'care and maintenance' basis, the 8th AF departed. During the next four months the enlarging of the airfield was

accomplished, but not without mishap. Whilst the runway was being resurfaced with the aid of a bitumen layer (which took only 252 man-hours), two members of an American Army Engineering Unit under the Officer Commanding, Capt Patton, fell into the boiling pitch. The accident was only noticed when their bones were reportedly spread over the runway and mixed in the solution.

On 18 November at 06.30hrs, Avro Anson Mk I, N5004, from No 10 OTU, RAF Abingdon, also came to grief. Whilst on a cross-country training flight from its base in Oxfordshire, its pilot, Sgt Lockhart, became lost in 10/10th cloud. He asked his wireless operator to call for assistance but, despite the wireless set being in good working order, he could not receive the control tower at Cheddington. Lockhart brought the Anson lower and circled the airfield beacon, but could not see a 'T' displayed to indicate the direction of the runway in use. He came lower but then saw red flares being fired from the control tower. Having no idea of the aircraft's location, and short of fuel, he ordered his crew to bale out, which they did without injury. Sgt Lockhart then crash-landed the Anson in an orchard at Hawkings Farm, Pitstone, just outside the 'Closed' airfield boundary.

By January 1943 the construction had been completed and the airfield was by then ready for operations, so the RAF transferred to No 2 Gliding School for Exercise 'Spartan'. This consisted of 15 officers and 120 other ranks who, despite bad weather, achieved 1,182 day-tows and 287 night-tows in the unit's Hotspur gliders, towed by their Miles Master Mk II tugs. Once the exercise had been completed, on 20 March 1943, the school moved to Weston-on-the-Green in Oxfordshire, and left the airfield vacant for its next occupants to move in.

———

Below:
A RAF pilot signs the obligatory Form 700 before taking a pupil up for a training flight in a Hotspur II training glider. The Hotspur was used primarily as an operational trainer with the Airborne Division.
IWM CH7883

Left:
Men of the 2901st CCRC Group sit around the stove that provided the warmth. The boxes on the floor provided heat in another form: chilli con carne. These men were the first Americans to arrive at Cheddington.
R. Dennison/113 Association

Far away in America, it had been a clear, crisp, blue sky that greeted five enlisted men from the US Army when they reported for duty at MacDill Field, Florida, in late October 1942. The privates, George Sweeny, Arny Van Heuvelen, Bill Weintraab, Henry Woolf and Johnny Wildman, were all fresh from Army Administration School and had been posted to MacDill to form the nucleus of a new Bomb Wing. Its Table of Organisation (TO) for staffing and rank structuring called for 45 officers and 130 enlisted men (EM), plus a signal company for communications. The Wing would be attached to the 3rd AF but was soon due to be reassigned to the 8th AF.

The first day of November saw the men in the new Bomb Wing treated, if one can use that term, to yet another parade. This one was more formal for it was the appointment of their Commanding Officer, Capt Garret C. Houseman. Within a few days of his appointment Capt Houseman received an influx of personnel and from them appointed 2Lt Robert Waite as Wing Adjutant, 2Lt Robert Moore as Commanding Officer Headquarters Squadron, and 2Lt Ira Reimer as Supply Officer. On 18 December Capt William McCaslin was appointed Assistant A-2, and two days later Maj Joseph Nate was posted in to take over command of the Wing from Capt Houseman. Maj Nate had been appointed CO several weeks earlier but had been on temporary duty at the Harrisburgh Intelligence School.

Maj Nate's wife, a 2Lt in the WACs, also arrived to spend Christmas with her husband. Christmas came, and despite the war all present had a marvellous time. The Major, who was expecting a posting for his unit at any moment, took full advantage of the interval. When the visit came to an end, he appointed an aircraft and crew from the Station Flight to fly his wife back to her unit, and accompanied her on the aircraft so as to be together for the extra few hours. The aircraft took-off and made for the Gulf of Mexico but, along with its crew and passengers, disappeared without trace. As a result of this loss, Capt Houseman became CO once more, but only for the short period to 10 March 1943, when Maj Oscar Steely arrived and assumed command.

For the Wing it was now time to enter the basic phase of overseas training, and the men were sent to specialist schools to prepare them for their subsequent work in the organisation. The majority of men had already attended training school once and were therefore engaged in an elaborate course of basic training with ample opportunities to apply all the knowledge they had previously acquired from their initial training. This included such subjects as chemical, desert and jungle warfare, map reading, extended and close order drill, commando tactics, protection against all methods of attack, field problems, first aid, field sanitation and general body conditioning, and forced marches both day and night in full pack. All this was quite unrelated to aviation, but it must be remembered that at this time the men were not attached to the Army Air Corps. During this training period more changes were made against staff officers; it was even reported that cash exchanged hands on a day-to-day basis as the enlisted men made bets on 'who would be boss today'. By the first week of May the constant changes had come to an end and had resulted in Capt McCaslin becoming Wing Adjutant; Lt Moore, Squadron Adjutant; Capt Hende, Squadron Commanding Officer; and Capt Houseman was back in command of the Wing.

The staff changes and completion of overseas training were just in time, for on 8 May 1943, having been alerted a week earlier, the Wing left by train for Camp Shanks, New York, on the initial stage of its long overseas journey. It arrived on the 10th and set up camp. In the days that followed, latrine rumours began to flow thick and fast: the men had no idea of their final overseas destination, even on the 23rd when they marched up the gang-plank of the liner *Mariposa*, which was berthed at Staten Island. Where were they going? Some said the South Pacific, others said Iceland, a few thought China, and one or two put forward England. The rest had no idea, but would not have been surprised if it had been Texas! However, Headquarters Army Air Corps had no doubt about the destination for the Wing, which by now had taken on the full title of the 20th Bomb Wing (Heavy), and its destination was to be England — in support of the daylight bombing of Germany.

On 1 June the *Mariposa* docked at Liverpool after her long Atlantic crossing. The officers and men of the 20th disembarked and boarded trains for their first English base at Headquarters VIII Bomber Command, High Wycombe. 'Pinetree' as the base was known, had taken over a girl's school and was set in a tree-shrouded area not far from the centre of town. This location,

30 miles from London was only four miles from RAF High Wycombe, Headquarters of RAF Bomber Command. The next few days were spent unloading bags, setting up home and being briefed about England and what to expect. The one thing the men were not told to expect was that Pinetree would be their home for just a week, for within seven days of arriving, 200 officers and men departed by truck convoy for a second change of base — the airfield at Cheddington.

Whilst the 20th Bomb Wing had been disembarking at Liverpool, the famous liner *Queen Mary*, which had previously brought over the 44th Bomb Group, was again crossing the 'Big Pond'. On board was another cargo of men and machines, including **Sgt Bob Downs**. He remembers that crossing very well:

'Whilst on the voyage we were only given fresh water for drinking. For washing or bathing, we had to use salt water which was terrible. As a result, few if any of us did wash, and so it was with much relief that, on June 6th 1944, we berthed in Scotland. Orders were given to wash, then dress in our "first class" uniforms and heavy wool coats. After what seemed hours, further orders were given to board a small boat which took us ashore. As we landed, we were greeted by the sound of bagpipes and the sight of Red Cross girls giving out coffee and cakes. It was then time to board a train and we were off. Whilst the beautiful countryside passed by, the men became very boisterous with singing and gambling taking place. At about midnight, we arrived at a station and off-loaded. We were then told by a group of officers who had come to meet us that we were at Cheddington, England, and it would be our home. They sounded as though they liked the place, since they mentioned an abundance of girls! We collected our packs and barrack bags and lined up on the platform, to wait for transport to arrive from the motor pool. The bags were heavy and put a strain on our backs. To relieve it, some of us leaned back against the ticket office. Private Hoskins leaned too far and, as he went through the window bum first, became our unit's first casualty.'

Above:
B-24s attempt to evade accurate and heavy flak. Note the bizarre patterns traced in the foreground, presumably caught through the use of a fast camera shutter speed. *113 Association*

Once driven to the airfield, all the men who were from the 379th Service Squadron, 9th Station Complement Squadron, 1077th Signal Company and the 39th Service Group, set up home alongside those from the 20th Bomb Wing. There was now at Cheddington, for the first time, a complete structure to staff and run a combat airfield. The delay in this formation may well have caused frustration in many of the officers and men, and together with their uncertain future, may have cast a shadow of doubt on the ability of their Commanding General and his advisors. This lack of confidence was unfounded, for these moves were just one small part in the build-up and formation of what was to be the biggest air force ever assembled — 'The Mighty Eighth'.

Right:
Airfields referred to in the text.

II
TRAINING

B-17 Flying Fortress

From the early days of operations by the 8th AF in England it was accepted by the American commanders that there would be a requirement for American crews to adopt many of the British military procedures. This was to ensure the safety and effectiveness of those units which would be involved in combat. It was therefore an early priority for Gen Eaker, Commander General, US 8th AF, to establish a training programme in England, so a request was made via Washington for a Table of Organisation (TO) to form Combat Crew Replacement Centres (CCRC). At the same time, the British Government was asked for any available airfields on which to base these centres, the idea being to run them on the same lines as RAF OTUs. Whilst this TO was being formulated and the airfield request assessed, the role of Bovingdon airfield in Hertfordshire was changed from combat

to Fortress crew training. Bovingdon had been home for American combat crews from the 92nd Bomb Group, whose 325th, 326th, 327th and 407th Bomb Squadrons were known as 'Fame's Favoured Few'. These squadrons had all flown B-17Fs, but with the activation of the new CCRC they were exchanged for older B-17Es that had been used by the 97th Bomb Group at Polebrook. The 'E' models were then used by the 92nd staff to train all future Fortress crews for combat in Europe.

B-24 Liberator

During the winter period of 1942 and into early 1943, bomber crew training had been for Fortress crews in the main — this was only natural, as there were many Fortress Groups arriving in England, but only one Liberator Group. A second was due, but had been sent to North Africa on temporary duty. It did not take much foresight to see Liberator replacement crews would soon be

Left:
Bovingdon – General arrangement.

required, and so the June gathering of units at Cheddington was an ideal time and place to form the first Liberator CCRC. In less than a month, staff from the Ordnance, Quartermaster, Signal Company, Service Squadron, Station Complement Squadron and Headquarters Squadron, reported for duty and 12 CCRC was activated. Maj Robert Grandmontagne, who had been at Bovingdon, was appointed Director of Training, and Maj 'Podge' Reed was appointed as the Base Commander. Maj Reed became ill and was admitted to hospital and, as a temporary measure Maj Grandmontagne assumed command of the Base, as well as keeping his other duties. He acted in this role until 21 August, when a Col Taylor, who was also from Bovingdon, arrived and assumed command.

At 12.00hrs on 16 August 1943, the RAF Ensign was lowered and replaced by the American 'Stars and Stripes' when the airfield handover service took place and the USAAF took control of the airfield. Everyone on the station had given what assistance they could to help get the school underway, with the result that when

classes began on 13 July, the 19 crews present had a varied and intensive curriculum, which was divided into six subjects which covered: air & tactics, take-off checks, bombardment, gunnery, radio and intelligence.

The school instructors were former combat crew members, most of whom had completed a tour of 25 missions, and were well informed from personal experience of the latest developments in combat operations in the European Theatre of Operations (ETO). For the trainee crews who had just completed their basic training, the direct contact with men who had experienced what they themselves would soon be facing, and who knew most of the answers to their questions, was without doubt a bonus. As a result, 32 crews passed through in the first month of the school's operation.

On 4 September 1943 the TO designed for the operation of the school came through and was put into effect. The school designation was changed to the 2901st CCRC and had attached the 2904th Replacement & Training Squadron (RTS). Maj William Todd was appointed CO and Maj Grandmontagne appointed his Director of Training. The school designation changed again on 15 November, to the 2nd CCRC, with the 2nd RTS attached. The school was well equipped with an intelligence library, radio facilities, bombardment and navigational equipment, and a left-over from the 44th Bomb Group — one of its old B-24D Liberators. This was mounted on concrete plinths and used as a crew trainer.

Personnel

For pilots and co-pilots the course in air & tactics was divided into 15 subjects: Pre-op checks, briefing procedure, air-sea rescue, interphone control, enemy tactics, ditching equipment, bale-out/ crashes, flying control, W/T facilities, weather, lost procedure, crew co-ordination, formation flying, aerodrome lighting and engine operations.

Above:
The crew of a 392nd Bomb Group Liberator returns to Cheddington, the station where they were trained for combat.
N. Senter/113 Association

Right:
Liberators of the 453rd Bomb Group stream contrails in the cold upper atmosphere en route to the target. Hollywood film star James Stewart was the Group's Executive Officer.
113 Association

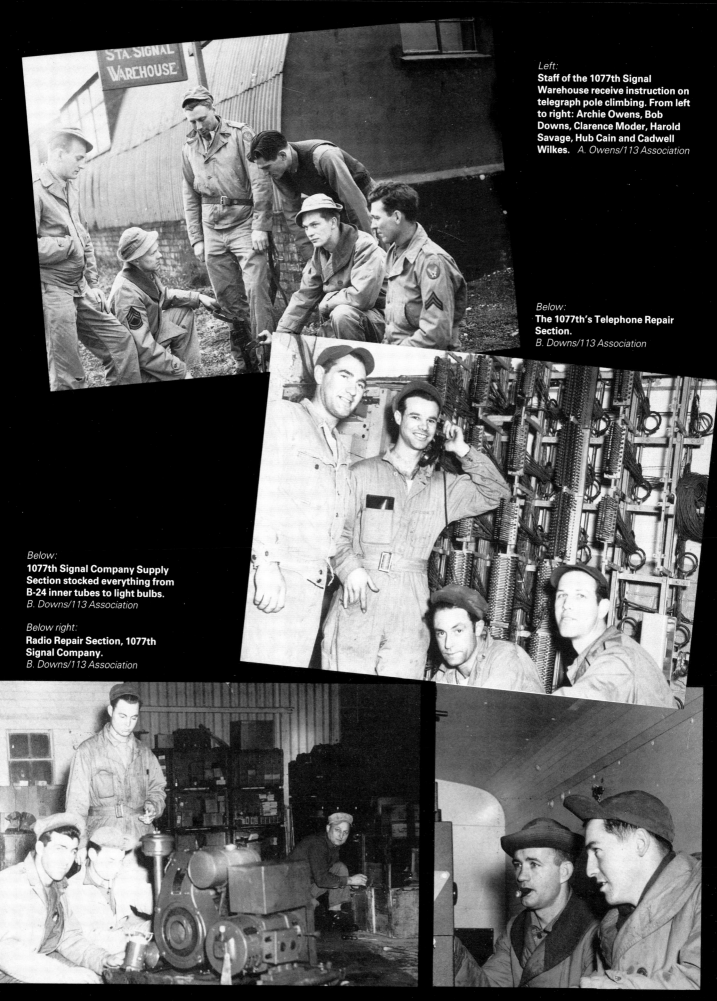

Left:
Staff of the 1077th Signal Warehouse receive instruction on telegraph pole climbing. From left to right: Archie Owens, Bob Downs, Clarence Moder, Harold Savage, Hub Cain and Cadwell Wilkes. *A. Owens/113 Association*

Below:
The 1077th's Telephone Repair Section.
B. Downs/113 Association

Below:
1077th Signal Company Supply Section stocked everything from B-24 inner tubes to light bulbs.
B. Downs/113 Association

Below right:
Radio Repair Section, 1077th Signal Company.
B. Downs/113 Association

Left:
Ward B, Cheddington Station Hospital photographed in November 1943.
L. Walck/113 Association

Below:
Sgts Adams and Scavatto hold morning Sick Call in July 1944.
L. Walck/113 Association

REPORT HERE FOR SICK

Left:
Sgt Helon makes up a tonic in the Station Pharmacy, July 1944.
L. Walck/113 Association

and landed at Bovingdon — from where its passengers were trucked to Cheddington, arriving at 15.30hrs. For the convoy, its journey was longer. After the crossing to Stranraer, it was a tiring trek to Cheddington via Carlisle, Preston and Lutterworth. It was escorted by MPs and each night stopped at a transit camp. The convoy arrived at its new home at noon on the 17th. As for the move of the CCRC to Ireland, this had taken place on 14 February when the staff, along with their 10 B-24Ds, left for Station 238 Cluntoe.

Responsibilities

When established on Site 4 at Cheddington, the staff of Composite Command set out to do their best with what they had. A Directive from 8th AF Headquarters and addressed to the Commanding General, outlined his Command responsibilities as follows: control of all Heavy Bombardment CCRC Groups for the 8th AF; operation and control of pre-combat training centres for fighter pilots for the 8th AF; pre-combat training of crews and personnel for the 9th AF; operation and maintenance of Gunnery Training Establishments for aerial gunners, and gunners to man defensive ground gun positions; administrative control and general court-martial jurisdiction over all units and establishments assigned to the 8th AF Composite Command — to sort out the bad boys! Supervision and control of off-station discipline by Military Police District 'B'; research, development, experimentation, and training on H2X radar; and operation and control of the 492nd Bomb Group at Alconbury in Huntingdonshire, who were on 'Pathfinder' operations.

The Command had also been instructed to make plans to absorb the operation and control of all Rest and Recuperative homes (R&R); to operate and supervise all units and functions which were not suitable for direct Air Force supervision, or assignment to either Fighter or Bomber Command. As if that was not enough, it was required to provide accommodation at Cheddington from time to time for any Bombardment Group that required revitalising, or a home whilst forming. It did not take long for this provision to be required, not by a Bomb Group, but a new Wing that would be commanded by a Very Important Person!

On 20 February 1944, orders were given by HQ 8th AF for a number of unit changes to take place. In the main these required

the staff from the 5th and 6th CCRC at Station 240 Mullaghmore, Northern Ireland, to be transferred to the 77th Station Complement Squadron. The unit designations were then transferred to Cheddington with the equipment trucked first to Station 237, then flown over to Cheddington on the 29th. What was the purpose of these moves? Answer: the formation at Cheddington on the 23rd, of the 8th Reconnaissance Wing (P), commanded by Elliott Roosevelt, son of the American President.

On 4 March, three provisional squadrons were formed under the Wing. The 8th Weather Squadron (Heavy), the 8th Weather Squadron (Light) and the 8th Courier Reconnaissance Squadron (Special). Within a few days 10 B-17Fs moved in, followed by P-38 Lightnings from the 50th Fighter Squadron (Twin Engine), from Iceland. The crews were then trained on British de Havilland Mosquito Mk XVIs by de Havilland staff and RAF personnel, a task that, due to the strange system of foot-operated brakes and steering, caused many unusual landing sights! After a few more weeks, the 8th Reconnaissance Squadron (Special) with B-17Fs, three Vultee L-5B Sentinel and six Noorduyn UC-64 Norseman aircraft, took over the work of the Courier Squadron, which was then disbanded. As these squadrons were now floating and in need of a Group Headquarters, the 8th Reconnaissance Group (Special) was formed on 22 March. Shortly thereafter the name was changed to that of the 802nd Reconnaissance Group (Special) (P), and in April the Group with its provisional squadrons and aircraft moved to Watton in Norfolk. The Wing HQ moved to 8th AF Headquarters, High Wycombe. In August, the Wing became the 325th Photo Wing (Reconnaissance), and the 802nd Reconnaissance Group (P) became the 25th Bomb Group. As for its squadrons, they became:

8th Weather Reconnaissance Sqn (H) (P) = 652nd Bomb Squadron (H)
8th Weather Reconnaissance Sqn (L) (P) = 653rd Bomb Squadron (L)
8th Reconnaissance Squadron (Special) = 654th Bomb Squadron (L)

Assigned Units

The next few months at Cheddington, in more ways than one, were a short hiatus in its development. Composite Command was well and truly dug-in. The men on the airfield could reaffirm the term 'dug', for digging became the order of the day. Whether it had been trenches for cables, trenches for gun or blast shelters, or just plain trenches, it was dig, dig, dig. Col Crisp, the new Station Commander, set about a station beautification programme which involved members of the Base performing pick and shovel details, clearing up areas, and laying down concrete walks. In order to accomplish this work, staff were confined to the Base, and performed these tasks for two to three hours in the evenings. This was after their regular duties had been completed! In conjunction with the beautification programme, a basic training programme was inaugurated which featured close-order drill, the manual of arms, firing on the range and lectures on chemical warfare. The beautification details came to an end when it became clear that the laying of paths had made the airfield more obvious to the enemy from the air. As for the lectures on explosives, they came to an abrupt end for the two instructors, Lt Louis Sherman and Sgt William Daugherty, when they were killed demonstrating to a class the method of handling incendiary bombs on 4 April 1944. Both men were from the 9th Station Complement Squadron. The 9th had also provided personnel to man the Motor Pool, Flying Control, Chemical Warfare, Fire and Crash Crew Sections, plus the Radio Direction-Finder (RDF) stations which were located just outside the base in Wilstone village.

The one thing the base did not have was women. This situation was improved on 23 May when, following a visit by two Womens Army Corps (WAC) officers from HQ 8th AF, a detachment of 56 enlisted women and two officers arrived. The detachment was commanded by Capt Marjorie Hunt, and took over the duties of some of the men in the Adjutant General, Headquarters, Transport, Medical, Engineering, A1, A2, A3 and A4 sections, plus the Link trainer. All the WACs had been in service for at least 17 months and were all volunteers for overseas duty.

On 1 May, an organisation known as the '8th Air Force Personal Equipment School' moved in on detached service from 'Pinetree'. Its headquarters were on the Technical Site. The instructors at the school were two officers and 10 enlisted men in the Officers' Section, and one officer and one enlisted man in the Enlisted Men's section, there being two schools in operation. Capt Dick Truckman was CO and instructed the Officer's School, assisted by

Top left:
As well as the radio equipment, 1077th men also had to keep their hands in with .50in gun turrets.
B. Downs/113 Association

Centre left:
Lee Roy Sullivan issues a B-24 inner tube from Station Supply.
N. Senter/113 Association

Bottom left:
Luther Walck of the 282nd Medical Dispensary poses beside an ambulance.
L. Walck/113 Association

Above:
Staff of the 282nd Medical Dispensary. Maj Winslow (seated, centre) took his own life with a pistol shortly before he was due to return to America.
L. Walck/113 Association

Right:
Terry O'Lean and Luther Walck of the 282nd Medical Dispensary 'snapped' off-duty in Aylesbury with the local Bobby.
L. Walck/113 Association

Lt Milton Mazer and Lt Robert Bender, who both instructed the enlisted men.

Officers and men attending the schools were from Heavy, or Medium Bomb Groups or Fighter Groups. On completion of the course, the officers became Personal Equipment Officers at their own stations and the enlisted men carried out the maintenance on the equipment. The course varied according to whether the students came from Heavy or Medium Bomb or Fighter Groups. For the Heavy it was of two weeks' duration, Medium five days, and for Fighter Groups one week. Training was in the use of oxygen equipment, maintenance of parachutes, flying clothing, air-sea rescue equipment, flak suits and dinghies of various types.

On 4 June another organisation moved in without aircraft, and was known as the 'Air Crew Evaluation & Research Detachment'. It was composed of six officers and 15 enlisted men, and was inaugurated by Gen H. H. Arnold, Chief of Staff of the USAAF. Its mission was divided into three phases.

● The training and classification test records of personnel assigned to Bomb Groups in the 8th AF were to be collated from basic AF Training Command records, which had been compiled for the detachment. The records were then to be compared with the combat performance of men in key assignments such as lead crew, to determine the value of the records to Squadron and Group Commanders in selecting men.
● To supplement the detachment's existing records by developing and administering to appropriate personnel, certain new tests devised as a result of the survey, and then to validate them against combat performance.
● With the findings from the above work, its task would be to revise and develop tests for the purpose of predicting combat performance, as accurately as possible, at the time aircrew entered operational training units.

The whole idea was that the classification personnel in America would be able to predict, with a high degree of accuracy, which men would make the best lead bombardiers, navigators and pilots. When the evaluation was completed the detachment left Cheddington and presented its findings to Gen Arnold.

In only four months Cheddington had been fully staffed, cleaned, painted and prepared. But what about aircraft? It is true that when the CCRC with its Liberators left, there followed a stream of units with aircraft, but only for short periods. First the Weather Squadron, then the Reconnaissance Wing and then the Courier Squadron, and last but not least, excitement was caused by the arrival of the 788th and 850th Bomb Squadrons, 801st Bomb Group, who were training to supply equipment and agents to resistance groups in Europe on 'Carpetbagger' missions. After initial training, their move out left Composite Command poised for its next task, and the airfield at Cheddington ready for more action. But, with the D-Day landings less than one month away, there were no aircraft to be found on the airfield, let alone a combat unit. But that situation would soon change.

Below:
Capt E. J. Winner, the 9th Station Complement Squadron CO, on duty for the Pay Parade. He is guarded by Sgt Grover Goins and assisted by 1Sgt Vester. Capt Winner was a veteran of the ill-fated Dieppe raid in August 1942. *N. Senter/113 Association*

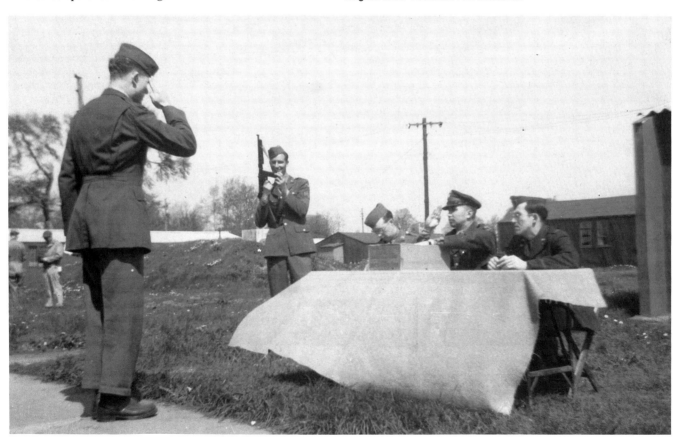

IV
THE MOUTH OF
PSYWAR

Chelveston and Night Leaflet Missions

Psychological warfare — or PsyWar — can claim to be a major force in proving the theory that 'the pen is mightier than the sword', for the clever use of propaganda leaflets, dropped from aircraft, was one of the most effective means of waging psywar during World War 2. This method of delivering messages, information or news was used in every theatre of operations and with considerable success. But Western Europe, with its many large centres of population and concentrations of Allied troops, promised the Allied leaders one of their greatest returns from the leaflets. There were two types of leaflet: 'whites' — true and from

the Allies to friend or foe in enemy occupied areas; or 'black' — claimed to be of enemy origination and for the enemy.

Leaflet or 'Nickeling' missions had been initiated from England by the RAF with a small mission over Kiel on the night of 3 September 1939, and gathered momentum as the war progressed. This type of operation had its opponents however, who thought supplying the enemy with 'toilet paper' to be a waste of resources. Some military commanders refused to accept the idea for a number of years, and a letter from AVM 'Bomber' Harris to AVM N. H. Bottomley dated 25 March 1942, in answer to a request for more leaflet operations, showed he had still not been convinced:

Left:
**Chelveston –
General arrangement.**

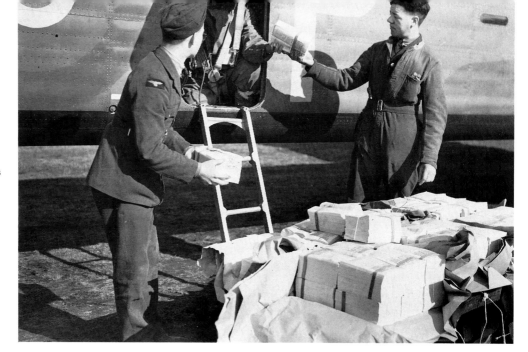

Right:
RAF groundcrews load leaflet bundles into a Whitley of No 102 Squadron early in the war. *IWM C912*

Below right:
A RAF aircrew member splits open the leaflet bundles prior to putting them down the Whitley's flare shute. *IWM C838*

'Can something please now be done to curb and keep within bounds these uncorrelated and enthusiastic attempts to shower rubbish all over the world at the expense of the bomber effort.

'If it takes 31 tons of nickels to explain to the French why we bombed Renault's, all I can say is that it is a pity we didn't add another 31 tons, drop them in bundles on Renault's, and thereby save the HE which it took to do the damage.

'When it comes to dropping tea, Christmas presents, and Easter eggs, things have really gone too far. Something must now really be done to stop this growing urge of the exiled governments and individual busybodies with idle hands, to play games in wartime when we are more than too busy on serious things.

'I will not drop tea or Easter eggs anywhere unless you guarantee that the packages are lethal.

'The only people likely to be affected by nickles are morons. Notoriously, morons are unable ro read. The only people who are likely to get the Easter eggs are the Gestapo, and why the devil should we feed them Easter eggs? How about quit foolin' and getting on with the war? These jesters are getting completely out of hand and it is high time someone put a heavy foot on them — or behind them. I'm not cross, but I damn soon will be.'

The involvement of the 8th AF with leaflet operations came as a result of just one telegram, number 462, sent on 28 May 1943 by Maj-Gen Ira Eaker to VIII Bomber Command and for action by its three Bombardment Wings. It requested: 'Desire you initiate leaflet-dropping operations as soon as possible.' Thus, for just one piece of paper, an operation was activated that produced and disseminated billions more.

Prior to this telegram, a visit was made by Col Bacon, A-2 of the 8th AF, to the RAF in late August 1942. The visit resulted in Bacon's G-2, Col James Childers, making an exploratory investigation into the RAF leaflet operations. He concluded on return: 'The RAF and PWE have worked out a system for producing leaflets very rapidly. With a simpler organisation, American leaflets should be produced even faster.' He submitted his report in September and requested that immediate arrangements be made to drop propaganda leaflets on bombing missions. The reply from A-3, VIII Bomber Command, was that 'It is wholly impractical to attempt to drop leaflets in loose form from a close formation of aeroplanes, since they would collect in the engine intake and radiators of other aeroplanes, forcing them to land'. This reply, however, put forward a suggestion that a device be developed that would hold the leaflets intact, and only release them when they had dropped below the bomber formations and as they approached the ground. This advice was accepted, and, as a result the A-2 VIII Bomber Command directed the Air Force Engineering Base Air Depot at Burtonwood (BAD 1) to undertake research into such a suitable device.

In a short time BAD 1 had come up with the answer. The leaflets would be tied in bundles by string and as the bundle dropped through the air, the increase in pressure would operate a simple aneroid barometer. This would operate at a desired height by collapsing a set of bellows, whose action would activate a catch releasing a small pin holding the two ends of string, thus allowing the bundle to break open. It was agreed to manufacture 50 test releases that, when attached to the bundles, would be stowed in large plywood boxes. These were to be hung upside down in the bomb bay, with their lids attached by chain to standard bomb shackles. When operated by the bombardier, the lids would swing open, releasing four bundles each containing 16,000 leaflets.

Work started in October, but was held up due to problems with the bellows in the aneroids which had to be redesigned. Research was accelerated again in the first part of March 1943 with flight testing of the complete device held on the 31st. Eight releases of

the containers were made and all were satisfactory, with the bundles clearing the aircraft from both the front and rear bomb racks. The fuses, set for 5,000ft, worked as planned and 25,000 leaflets were released from just one carrier, covering an area of half-a-mile by four miles (in the prevailing 25mph wind). The Development Committee accepted the device and, since the box was light (122lb when full), agreed it could be hung above a regular bomb load without affecting it and therefore no additional aircraft would be required for leaflet missions. It also made a number of other proposals, namely:

● That a Heavy Bombardment Group be designated to conduct further tests from operational altitudes, using a bomb-sight to determine limits of accuracy obtainable, and approximate area of coverage. A crew must be chosen who will take an interest in the development of this equipment.

● If the Office of War Information (OWI) indicates that a large quantity of leaflets will have to be dropped apart from on bombardment missions or on special occasions, it is recommended that development be extended to fighter-type aircraft where containers could be mounted on external bomb racks and less equipment and personnel will thereby be jeopardised.

● That an officer be designated by 8th Air Force to follow through on the development and act as Liaison Officer between the OWI and the operational units.

Maj-Gen Eaker acted on the recommendations and expressed his desire in a letter to the Commanding General of VIII Bomber Command 'to have one Heavy Bombardment Squadron equipped and trained immediately for the purpose of dropping leaflets'.

It may have been Eaker's desire to have a squadron devoted to leaflet dropping, but over the next few months there was no Command decision made as to whether leaflet missions for the OWI was going to be the sole task for a special squadron, or

Below:
USF124: L'Amérique en Guerre
Issue 109 of the French newspaper 'America in the War'. It was disseminated from 9 July to 7 August 1944. There was a total of 114 issues printed, but the first seventeen issues were not disseminated, the first being the 28/29 November 1942 copy.

Below right:
ZH1: Eisenhowers Statement
A joint statement signed by Dwight D. Eisenhower and the Dutch Prime Minister Pieter Gerbrandy. It was dropped over Holland on D-Day by NLS Fortresses, and advised the civilians of the D-Day landings.

whether it would be a mission all Bomber Groups operating over Germany would perform. The answer came in a confidential telegram sent by 8th AF to VIII Bomber Command, dated 28 May 1943, which raised just as many questions as it answered. It did, however, give an outline of the basic objectives of a leaflet programme and an indication of a starting date by stating 'desire you initiate leaflet dropping operations as soon as possible'. It also made clear that there would be two types of operations, both having a strict condition: daylight leaflet dropping in conjunction with heavy bomber raids on targets in Germany. The load desired was for each aeroplane to carry the maximum number of leaflets possible in addition to its existing bomb-load. Night leaflet dropping by B-24s that were at this stage being readied for this type of operation. No leaflets were to be carried by heavy bombers attacking occupied countries.

On paper, for the first time, was the 'way ahead'. It was requested that the 'scale of operations desired is maximum employment of aeroplanes, consistent with ability to maintain availability of operational crews, and a proper standard of maintenance'. Four areas were named for the operations: the Paris area with 7½ tons per week; the industrial north of France including Lille, Cambrai, Roubaix, Douai and Valenciennes; the South of France including the cities of Lyons, Bordeaux, Dijon, Toulouse and Marseilles; and Holland.

To overcome a number of operating problems, including the fact that certain bombs (1,000 and 1,600lb) would not fit in bomb bays with the leaflet boxes, a meeting was held on 4 June, chaired by Col Ordway, A-2 8th AF. Present also were other representatives from A-2, A-3 and A-4 sections. The outcome was successful with a number of problems being solved, including the comment that leaflets should be placed in the last aircraft of each Group to prevent the bundles hitting any other aircraft. Minutes of this meeting were issued, and resulted in a directive from VIII Bomber Command to the Commanding Generals of the Bomb Wings on 10 July, entitled 'Leaflets'. It ratified all the proposals and recommendations that had been made to date and set out the

Message urgent

du Commandement Suprême des Forces Expéditionnaires Alliées

AUX HABITANTS DE CETTE VILLE

Afin que l'ennemi commun soit vaincu, les Armées de l'Air Alliées vont attaquer tous les centres de transports ainsi que toutes les voies et moyens de communications vitaux pour l'ennemi.

Des ordres à cet effet ont été donnés.

Vous qui lisez ce tract, vous vous trouvez dans ou près d'un centre essentiel à l'ennemi pour le mouvement de ses troupes et de son matériel. L'objectif vital près duquel vous vous trouvez va être attaqué incessament.

Il faut sans délai vous éloigner, avec votre famille, pendant quelques jours, de la zone de danger où vous vous trouvez.

N'encombrez pas les routes. Dispersez-vous dans la campagne, autant que possible.

PARTEZ SUR LE CHAMP !
VOUS N'AVEZ PAS UNE MINUTE A PERDRE !

Z.F.4

S.A 182
ROMILLY SUR SEINE

Above:
ZF4: Warning Message
On the eve of D-Day, 6 June 1944, the first Allied aircraft to cross the enemy beachhead were Leaflet Squadron aircraft, which dropped copies of ZF4 over France. This leaflet warned of an impending invasion.

Left:
The 305th Bomb Group's first daylight raid was to Romilly Sur Seine in France on 20 December 1942. A Mosquito of No 540 Squadron RAF photographed the bomb hits after the raid.
Crown Copyright

Top right:
Dan Brennan (third from left) served with the RAF before joining the 8th AF. He is pictured here during training on Whitleys with No 10 OTU at RAF Abingdon.
D. Brennan/113 Association

Above right:
***Foolish Virgin,* 42-30822 the B-17F that Dan Brennan trained on.** *D. Brennan/113 Association*

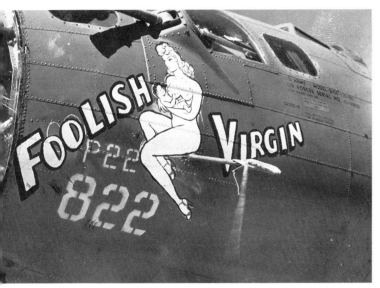

policy to be adhered to, but with a major change contained in proposal 3.

Bomb Wings were to carry leaflets on ALL raids over Germany — therefore operational units would carry on the task; once the initial supply of leaflets had been used the Bomb Groups would have to reorder off their own backs; leaflets were to be carried in the last THREE aircraft of each Bomb Group formation; bombardiers were responsible for seeing that the boxes were hung correctly, and that as the boxes were to be placed on top of bomb racks, they could not be dropped until the normal bomb-load had been released.

This letter not only outlined the policy, but requested that the 1st and 4th Bomb Wings provide the designation of those Bomb Groups which would perform the task. Within 48hr the Groups had been selected and were, for the 1st Bombardment Wing, the 91st, 92nd, 303rd and 305th Bomb Groups; and for the 4th Bombardment Wing, the 95th, 390th and 100th Bomb Groups. However, due to problems in obtaining the required equipment, only five of the Groups were ready for operations by 23 July.

The first leaflet mission to Germany, in conjunction with a daylight bombing raid, took place on 28 July 1943 with aircraft selected from the 1st Bombardment Wing's 91st, 303rd, 305th and 306th Bomb Group, plus aircraft from the 4th Bombardment Wing. These aircraft were loaded with 273,000 leaflets which were dropped successfully. The following day with the addition of aircraft from the 92nd Bomb Group at Bovingdon, which were

substituted for those of the 303rd at Molesworth, nearly three times as many leaflets were disseminated. From August to mid-September however, only four leaflet missions were flown and thus the 8th AF commitment of 45,000lb per week was far from being achieved. In an attempt to overcome this failure, a directive from VIII Bomber Command to HQ 1st Air Division on 20 September, directed that the 422nd Bomb Squadron prepare six aircraft 'to carry out extensive leaflet operations at night over Germany and occupied countries as soon after October 1st as practicable'. As a result of this directive, by the end of December 1943, the 8th AF was able to report that leaflet operations had shown a substantial improvement, with 18 missions in the month being tasked and completed. These missions had distributed a total of 21 million leaflets to Germany, pamphlets for Belgium, and copies of *L'Amérique* to France and had ensured that the commitment of 45,000lb per week now had been exceeded!

But why was the 422nd Bomb Squadron selected to drop these leaflets at night, and not bombs by day — the task that it had been trained for? For the planners the decision had been an easy and obvious one.

In September 1943, the 422nd Bomb Squadron, which was one of four squadrons attached to the 305th Bomb Group based at Chelveston, Northants, was ordered to undergo intensive training for night operations. The objective was to use its combat crews as 'Pathfinder' or 'Lead Crews' on night bombing missions by the 8th AF. As the 8th AF had been tasked as a day bomber force, its crews or aircraft had not been trained or equipped for night operations. To rectify this situation and make the 422nd Squadron's aircraft suitable for night-time flying, the 305th Engineering Section was engaged in an arduous programme of design, modification and installation.

In all the squadron's assigned aircraft, the sheet-metal workers installed astrodomes that had been taken from wrecked aircraft, and mounted them on racks constructed from salvage; astro compass installations were also completed in the same way. New and larger navigation tables were installed to accommodate the projections from the ceiling-mounted astrographs. The Instrument Section went to work and rewired the new navigational equipment to the existing equipment, moved instrument panels and rearranged the cabin lighting. It also fitted dead-reckoning compasses and hung special goose-neck lights. New radio antennae, direction-finding and Gee equipment units were installed by the Radio Section. Much of the new equipment required rearrangement of existing compartments for it to fit. Blackout curtains, to separate the navigator's and bombardier's rooms, were found to be necessary and a 1½in black stripe was painted outside the aircraft around the edge of each window. This was to prevent light leakage at the edge of the blackout curtains. All unpainted metal in the interior compartments was painted black to reduce reflection and glare from ground searchlights. Most of the interior surfaces of the waist and tail sections of the fuselage were likewise blackened and had the outside windows painted over so that, in case of any emergency, the dome lights could be turned on without the danger of any light escaping. On six aircraft it was found necessary to replace all the instrument dials whose luminous paint had deteriorated. Red instrument lighting rather than the former blue light, which could be so injurious to night vision, was substituted. New tail lights, interior warning lights, flare pistol sockets and demand oxygen systems were also installed and the bomb bay warning lights on the tail were removed. Flame suppressors, to dampen the light from engine exhaust flames, were fitted on all engines. Also, normal running lights were replaced by English 'resin' lights, which were installed in the same place.

The Engineering and Instrument Sections were not the only departments to be given modification work to carry out. The Armoury had to build fire cut-off cams into the gun ports, to prevent the now 'blinded' gunners from firing their guns into the tail or wings of their own aircraft during any defensive action. To suppress the flames created when the guns were fired, 'flash hiders' were likewise placed on all the 0.5in calibre guns. The camera doors were baffled and safety belts for gunners and rear crewmen fitted. All microphone switches, oxygen connections, heating suit junctions and first-aid points were marked faintly with luminous paint. The undersides of the aircraft were painted in a thick coat of gloss black to 'cone-out' searchlights from the ground. Along with the squadron code 'JJ' on the fuselage, the 305th Bomb Group 'triangle G' was painted on the tail. Last, but not least, discreet nose art was liberally applied on many of the B-17s — if selected by the crew and crew chief.

With the modification work completed and the aircraft poised for action, the only thing left to finish was that of crew training for the night missions. Lt Truesdell, the Assistant Operations Officer, must take a lot of credit for this because he designed a night training syllabus for the squadron after liaising with the RAF. It was a great loss when the squadron received news of his untimely death. At 23.30hrs on 31 August, whilst on a training flight over Foulsham in Norfolk, his B-17F, 42-5376 *Eager Eagle* had collided head-on with an RAF Bristol Beaufighter. There were 11 crew on board the Fortress, including a RAF officer, but only two survived. These were the two waist gunners who had baled out.

On completion of the intensive ground and flight training, it was agreed to send the crews to accompany RAF aircraft on a few night bombing missions; the idea was for the American crews to gain actual night combat experience. The first of these joint raids took place on 8 September 1943, when five Fortress aircraft bombed Boulogne. The raid was recorded in the 422nd Squadron records: '23 officers and 30 enlisted men wrote a new chapter in the 8th AF and 422nd Bomb Squadron part in World War 2. Taking-off in 41-24514 *We The People*, Maj Price led his Squadron in the 1st Night Attack on the Enemy, in a Fortress.'

By mid-September the squadron had completed its third 'Secret' night bombing mission over France — the most distant to date — and within five miles of the Italian border. The crews had taken the bit in their teeth with the new task and by October had completed a further three missions. Each mission included a mass take-off from Chelveston, then flying separately the briefed course and timed schedule to the target. Bombing was to be aimed with the help of target indicators that had been dropped previously by RAF Pathfinder aircraft which had been leading the raid.

A total of 35 aircraft were dispatched up to the squadron's eighth raid on 4 October, 32 being effective and two aircraft reported as lost, missing in action. The first, 42-2955 *Centaur*, a B-17F coded JJ-D and flown by Capt Harvey B. Rogers was reported on the 27 as 'coned' over the target area, and going down smoking in a wide spin. The second was on 2 October and was another B-17F, serial 42-3091 JJ-H, and flown by Lt Thomas S. Seay. *Centaur* was the first B-17 lost at night by the 8th AF during World War 2.

Following the results of these first few missions, the 8th AF decided to terminate night bombing operations. The training and effort put in by the 422nd aircrews had not been in vain, however, for the Air Force Planners decided that the squadron was the obvious choice for a new task. With the experience it had gained, it could perfect and use to full advantage the equipment required to fulfill the leaflet distribution requirements of the 8th AF. Thus,

for the 422nd, night bombing missions were slowly replaced by missions whose bomb-loads changed from bomb, to bomb-and-leaflet, then to those of just leaflet. The first solely-leaflet raid was the squadron's ninth night mission, flown on 7 November 1943, and recorded in the unit's diary as follows: 'The mission was a morale builder for the French, using the theory that "The pen is mightier than the sword" — our aircraft carried leaflets instead of bombs.'

When the aircraft left Chelveston for France, an air raid was in progress with a 'Red' showing. When the squadron reached London, which was also on a 'Red', it was fired upon by Allied guns but thankfully without any hits being scored. A natural progression from targets in France was to Germany, and so on the squadron's 24th night mission, which took place on the 30th, eight Fortress aircraft dropped leaflets over German targets.

The year of 1944 saw the airfield at Chelveston become a hive of activity, but for the 422nd which had crews flying bombing missions by day and leaflet missions by night, the continuous pressure of both types of mission began to show. Following a period as Operations Officer, the new CO, **Maj Aber**, who had assumed command on 26 November, recorded in his diary:

'An eventful but hectic day for the squadron. Last night during our initial orientation lecture to the new crews, an alert came through for six Pathfinder aircraft. I had not anticipated this — crews had never flown these aircraft nor met their "Mickey" operators. Even so, with considerable rush, the various sections swung into action. Around 03.00hr, after a short briefing, the six ships took off to their Groups to lead the combat Wings. The target was Berlin. One ship aborted. Stood down the next day so had a chance to meet the crews and test some aircraft. Thirty-three crews in the squadron. Group will have thirty in the other three squadrons combined, which just about makes this the 422nd Group.'

If Maj Aber believed his squadron to be overworked, he was not alone in his thoughts. With his Pathfinder crews proving their worth during the day and his remaining crews flying leaflet missions at night, his commanders were looking at his over-tasked squadron, and seeking a solution. In May they transferred 12 422nd Pathfinder crews from the squadron to Bassingbourn, which left the leaflet crews time to sort themselves out. Maj Aber, who had been busy with the development of leaflet bombs, packing procedures, and operational training, still found time to press for separation of his leaflet and Pathfinder crews. On 4 April he talked with the Deputy Commander General, 8th AF, and found that HQ in Washington would sanction authorisation for a separate squadron to be formed, solely for psychological warfare missions. On the 22nd, whilst at a commanders' meeting, he argued for the separation and gained the authorisation of 305th Bomb Group commander, Col Lawson. Now he had only to obtain Gen Williams' consent for the split to take place — and this he achieved.

Before the squadron separated, the crews flew a number of leaflet missions, one of the most important being on the night of 5 June 1944 — the eve of D-Day. Col Aber, together with 11 other crews, spearheaded Operation 'Overlord' and were the first Allied aircraft to cross the enemy beachhead. Singly and unescorted they dropped leaflets warning the people of 17 villages and cities in France, Belgium and Holland of the dangers of the imminent invasion.

On 9 June 1944, the Chief of Staff AFCC, Col Lee, received news that the 8th AF had decided his command would be assigned to the night leaflet activity, and that the unit was to be relocated at

This page:
On 12 May 1944, 50 officers and men flying in five aircraft took off on a leaflet mission to Denmark. B-17 42-31032 JJ-B, flown by Lt Michael, was attacked by a Junkers Ju 88 which killed its two waist gunners SSgts George Barber and Robert Walker. Both TSgt Louis Hatin the radio operator, and SSgt Nicholas Mastroianni the tail gunner were badly wounded. TSgt Dan Brennan the ball turret gunner also received serious injuries as a result of the attack but succeeded in beating off the Ju 88 before shooting it down. On return to the UK the B-17 landed at RAF Friston where the dead and injured were taken off the aircraft and the flak damage inspected. Note No 2 engine has been feathered.
B. Gunderson/113 Association

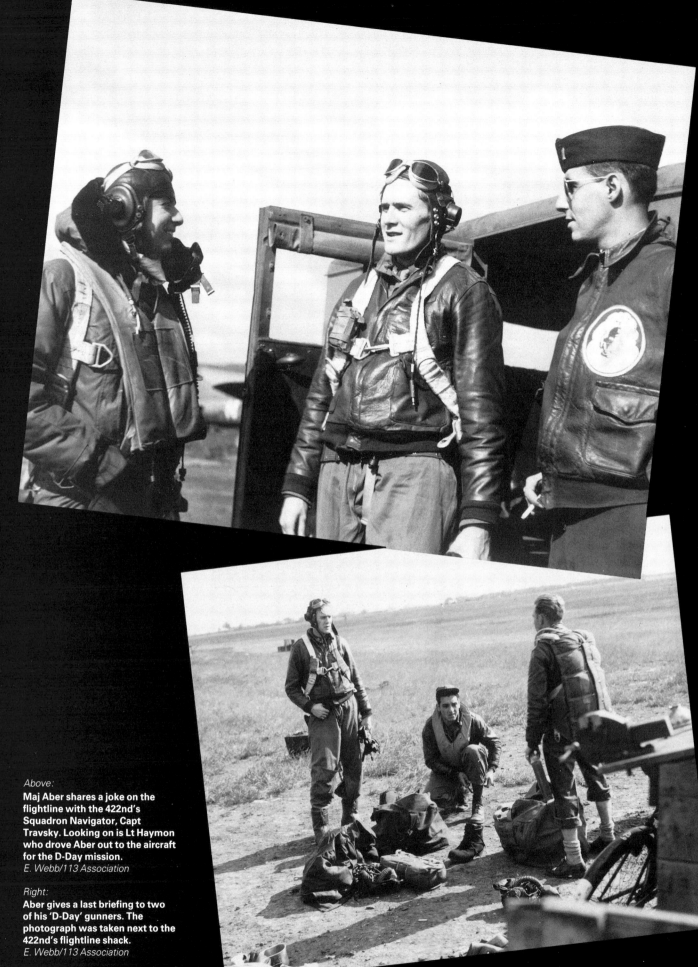

Above:
Maj Aber shares a joke on the flightline with the 422nd's Squadron Navigator, Capt Travsky. Looking on is Lt Haymon who drove Aber out to the aircraft for the D-Day mission.
E. Webb/113 Association

Right:
Aber gives a last briefing to two of his 'D-Day' gunners. The photograph was taken next to the 422nd's flightline shack.
E. Webb/113 Association

Cheddington. A requirement for dropping approximately 45,000lb of leaflets per week was prescribed, and with effect from 14 June 1944 the responsibility for specialised night leaflet dropping was assigned to AFCC.

Fourteen specially modified B-17 Flying Fortress aircraft, 14 trained combat crews and approximately 45 maintenance and operations personnel were to be transferred from the 1st Bomb Division for assignment to the 858th Bomb Squadron.

Field orders for night leaflet operations were to be issued by HQ 8th AF and the transmission of this information by scrambler telephone to the A-3 Duty Controller was to be the responsibility of HQ AFCC. This was to be transmitted at least 6hr before take-off and was to include information on targets, routes, altitudes and times. The targets themselves were to be selected by the Office of War Information in accordance with the official list of target priorities.

The AFCC's Flying Control was to be responsible for the clearance of all night leaflet aircraft and for all necessary arrangements for night flying aids, such as Pundits, Beacons and Occults. Mission flash reports were to be transmitted by scrambler telephone to the A-3 Duty Controller at HQ 8th AF, upon completion of each operational mission. These reports were also to be confirmed by teletype. The Office of War Information itself was to be responsible for the supply and delivery of leaflet bombs.

At this stage it was planned to eventually replace the B-17s currently in use with B-24 Liberators complete with trained crews.

As a result of this directive, the new squadron was formed by transferring the 858th Bomb Squadron to Cheddington on 21 June 1944, but leaving its combat crews, aircraft and other key operating personnel behind. The following Saturday, the 1st Air Division dispatched from the 422nd Bomb Squadron, Chelveston,

63 officers and 126 enlisted men who were experienced combat crews, plus five officers and 41 enlisted men from the maintenance section. The remainder of the men arrived on the 25th, with Maj Aber flying B-17G 43-37516 *Tondalayo*, the aircraft he would lose his life in eventually. The 422nd Squadron diary recorded: 'The six combat crews who stood-by at this station for last night's mission departed by aeroplane for Station 113. Maj Aber, flying 516, gave much-buzzed site No 6 its most memorable buzz-job by a B-17, as a farewell gesture.'

Once at Cheddington the staff of the newly-formed 858th Bomb Squadron along with its new CO, Maj Hambaugh, unpacked and, with their 13 B-17s, prepared for work. The next day at 21.00hrs the combat crews were called for a mission briefing, but due to bad weather the sortie was scrubbed. But, as crews would soon find out, the weather would have to be extremely bad for this to happen again — much worse than that for a normal bombing mission to be scrubbed!

The squadron's first mission from Cheddington was on 27 June when six aircraft took off at midnight for targets in Occupied France. During the remainder of the month a further 21 missions were flown to targets in France, Belgium and Holland, with the loss of just one aircraft. On 6 July B-17G 42-39811, with Lt Mann as pilot, was posted missing in action. On the 10th, there was a non-combat loss when Fortress '530', with Capt Weil as pilot, took off for a cross-country navigation training flight. Within minutes of take-off a fire broke out in a top turret oxygen pipe. Weil made a hasty landing at nearby RAF Halton, but despite the efforts of

Below:
All that was left of Fortress '530' after it caught fire on take-off from Cheddington. The firemen in the foreground were from Aylesbury.
B. Gunderson/113 Association

Above:

Pistol Packin' Mama **with air and groundcrews. One of the ground crew members can be seen still working on the port inner engine.**
113 Association

Left:

Pilot Dale Wilkes is pictured alongside his gloss-black painted B-24. Both day and night missions are painted below the pilot's window.
D. Wilkes/113 Association

the RAF and civil fire service the aircraft was burnt out. There were no serious injuries among the crew, despite Weil being struck by a propeller whilst leaving the wreck. However, the claim to fame as the unit's first true casualty whilst at Cheddington must go to Hulett Collins: he accidentally shot himself in the leg with a .45in pistol whilst on early evening guard duty on 3 August!

The Squadron HQ was located in an old Base Operations building, and the former Chemical Warfare building was used as the Intelligence Library. The aircraft being flown were also not new. In fact the squadron held a unique record, with four B-17s completing 103, 98, 95 and 91 missions; B-17F 42-30791, *Pistol Packin' Mama*, came top with only two aborts, and *Swing Shift* with no aborts and 95 missions to its credit came a close second.

After the Allied invasion of the Continent in June, greater emphasis had been placed on appeals to foreign workers to sabotage Germany's war efforts, and the futility of continued resistance by the German forces was also being played upon in propaganda. Furthermore, there was a change in propaganda policy which resulted in an increase in the total leaflets dropped. In June the 858th dropped 209.6 tons; July on 133 sorties 216.1 tons; and August, a further increase in sorties and of leaflets being dropped. To cope with the increases seven new crews from the 856th Bomb Squadron, 492nd Bomb Group, along with their Liberators, were put on DS at Cheddington. On the 13th, a further five crews were transferred in from the 36th Bomb Squadron and, like the 856th, has also been based at Harrington. The squadron's designation was also changed to that of the 406th Bomb Squadron (Night Leaflet). To complete the changes, Maj Earle J. Aber replaced Col Hambaugh as the new squadron CO, and had a total staff in his care of 80 officers and 387 enlisted men.

Fated Flights

Whilst on a night leaflet mission on 16 August and over the third of its five targets, Fortress 42-30791, flown by Lt Dick Bailey, suffered a fire in its No 1 engine. Dick cut the engine, feathered the propeller and then put the aircraft into a dive, levelling off at 23,000ft. This action extinguished the flames, but as he was still unable to maintain speed, he continued to let down to 15,000ft. At the same time he was engaged by an enemy aircraft, which attacked him from below and which had not been seen until it began to fire its guns. TSgt Charles Williams, the Fort's tail gunner, commenced firing immediately and called Dick to take evasive action to starboard. Dick's top gunner brought his guns to bear upon the enemy aircraft which exploded just as the Fort's gunner was about to open fire. There followed a tremendously bright flash, then pieces of the enemy aircraft could be felt hitting the Fort's fuselage. Charles was credited with one enemy aircraft destroyed and Fortress 791 *Pistol Packin' Mama*, had a swastika painted on her nose to record the 'kill'.

On the 18th, the squadron received news that was not so good and that came as a blow to all. B-24H 42-295238, coded J6-K (J6 having replaced JJ as the new squadron code), flown by Lt Chester Cherrington, was lost whilst on a high altitude cross-country training flight. The intended altitude was 14,000ft but, for some unknown reason, whilst flying at only 100ft the Liberator collided with a chimney at Burghill Mental Hospital (now St Mary's), near Hereford. The Liberator crashed in flames in the grounds of the hospital and was destroyed in the resulting fire. The crew of 10 were killed. At the time of the accident, visibility was two miles and the wind from the southwest, with a cloud-base of 600-800ft. The only indication of the cause of the crash came from the fact that one engine had been feathered prior to impact, indicating possible engine trouble.

Following September, when a total of 105 aircraft were dispatched with 1,050 leaflet bombs to 313 targets, October brought more work. A total of 144 aircraft were dispatched, all but one making it back to Cheddington. On the 12th, Liberator 42-39845 suffered an engine fire and the captain, Lt Shannon, gave the bale-out order. After being abandoned in flight, the aircraft crashed in flames near Rennes in France.

Right:
Herb with another NLS B-24, *Lady Grace*. *H. Trebing/113 Association*

Far right:
Chas Hurst, navigator; Ray Murray, bombardier; Lew Caulk, pilot; and Mat 'Vic' Vicovich, co-pilot, with *Shady Lady*. The one-inch black band around the windows was to prevent light leakage.
N. Senter/113 Association

November saw an extra seven crews and their aircraft arrive at Cheddington on Detached Service, to cope with the increase in pressure that was being put upon the NLS for more sorties. The crews were from the 856th Bomb Squadron, and had been on 'carpetbagger' missions (dropping supplies and agents to resistance forces), or 'Gas Runs' (missions with the bomb-bay full of fuel). It was no holiday for them at Cheddington, for after arrival on 6 November, they flew their first leaflet mission on the 8th. **Stan Seger** who was one of the pilots, noted in his diary at the time:

'Take-off: 21.45 hours; landed: 02.30 hours; target: Moulden, Germany. We had rockets fired at us over Chanes at 25,000 feet and flak at intervals over Belgium and Germany. Had trouble with bundles getting out and three were wedged in rear bomb-bay. Front right bomb-bay door was flying loose. Good weather at field, only ice formed was on windshield in traffic pattern, but runway was icy. All went well.'

On 15 November he was tasked for Duisberg in Germany and noted:

'No opposition in or out. Good weather except at Cheddington and was diverted to Oulton. We were weathered there for five days. Left November 20th at 11.00hrs. Lemke's crew took off the 18th and had to return to the field. On his turn on to the final approach, he made a vertical bank and "stalled out" and crashed.'

Murray Peden, who joined the RCAF and then completed a tour of operations with No 214 Squadron RAF, wrote in his book *A Thousand Shall Fall*:

'An American Liberator crew returned one afternoon from operations over Germany and landed at Oulton in the face of generally deteriorating weather. It was like the old times in the mess that night having a scattering of pinks around the bar. The weather kept on deteriorating, so with a full mess and some

warmly responsive guests, the party soared to memorable heights of hilarity. Next morning bright and early, the Americans were in the mess for breakfast, champing at the bit to get back down to the Flights and return to base. They rode up with us in the crew bus, and left us with a volley of friendly insults, in front of Flying Control. In twenty minutes they were all dead! They had taken off under a low ceiling and disappeared briefly into the cloud. Whether the pilot had then decided to make a circuit and try to get back to Oulton, no one will ever know. The Liberator suddenly reappeared, diving out of the cloud in a turn and crashed just beyond one of the maintenance hangars.'

One of the satisfying things about researching events from the past is that, with luck, you discover the background to what really happened. In this case research found that Peden was incorrect, and not all the crew were killed. **Jim Albright**, who was a member of Lt Fred Lemke's crew — the crew who were on the Liberator which Murray Peden saw, recalls:

'For the first time in all our flying as a crew, Les Cazzell, our engineer, and John Koliada, our waist gunner, started up the engines before our pilot and co-pilot climbed in. Immediately after take-off, I looked out the waist window and noticed petrol flowing down the wing near the number three engine, from an open fuel tank cap. I called the pilot who said he was aware of it, and that his main concern was the hot superchargers under the engine, at the trailing edge of the wing. In his last few words to us, he asked if we wanted him to try a landing, or take the aircraft higher for a bale-out. We all agreed on a landing. On the first two passes he was not lined up with the runway and had to try again. On the third attempt, he banked it very sharp and we just seemed to fall out of the sky. I tumbled around like I was in a clothes dryer, and my whole life seemed to pass by in a split second. After things settled down, I got to my knees and noticed an opening above me. I tried to pull myself out, but could not. Someone then "booted" me out, and I tumbled to the ground — I think it was Dan Bradley our

Left:
Herb Trebing with B-24 *Midnite Mistress*. *H. Trebing/113 Association*

navigator. I finally stumbled away from the wreck, but was stopped by someone who gave me morphine — well he tried!'.

When the aircraft hit the ground, the left wing struck first and was torn off, throwing the full weight of the aircraft on to the nose and forward fuselage. Lt Bradley, and Sgts Albright and Koliada who were in the waist section, and were the only survivors of the crash, all other crew members being killed instantly.

When the Operations Section at Harrington was informed that one of its aircraft had been involved in a crash, it took no action, for it had no aircraft detailed for missions or training, and was not in contact with those on DS at Cheddington. This presented problems, but they were soon resolved. There was more confusion, however, when Jim left hospital to return to

Cheddington. His mail had been marked 'Deceased' and was about to be returned to his wife. Also, with the exception of his flying jacket, all his clothing had been either returned to the Supplies Section, or was missing altogether!

The year 1944 came to a very cold, but successful end for the NLS. As it was stood down for two days over the Christmas period, a squadron party was held. Whilst the 'Sad Sacks' band under the musical direction of Rocco Savino played the night away, the men had chance to relax and forget the war for a while.

Whilst at Cheddington, 868 aircraft had been dispatched to 3,067 targets and only four had been lost: one on a training flight, one on take-off, one in flight and one when Lt Abernathy crashed on landing at Woodbridge, Suffolk, whilst returning from the last mission of his tour. The officers and men in the NLS felt happy with their results for 1944, but were soon brought back to reality by the first events in 1945. The New Year started with a loss — a big one at that — when on 3 January B-24H 42-52650, coded J6-E, crashed on take-off with the loss of Lt Ray Hendrix and his crew. An engine had cut and, due to the loss of power at a critical time the aircraft failed to climb and came down in an orchard to the west of the airfield at Buckland.

The next night, the Squadron Operations Section received a telephone call from a Capt Huffner at 'Pinetree', reporting that a Sgt Eaton, a gunner with Lt Bronar's Liberator crew, had baled out of his aircraft along with the rest of the crew. The aircraft had been coned by searchlights over the battle lines in Belgium and had been hit by flak. Sgt Eaton had walked all night until he came to airfield A-89, where he reported in. He thought the rest of the crew, who he had not been in contact with, were all safe.

Following the first tragedy on 3 January, there was nearly another on the 20th when a Liberator on a local training flight was struck by lightning. The aircraft went out of control and one

Below:
Overshadowed by Southend Hill, a Liberator is 'bombed-up' under the watchful eye of a guard. *H. Trebing/113 Association*

of the crew members, Lt Gilman Blake, baled out before the order had been given. He used the ditching exit in the topside of the fuselage, struck the tailplane of the aircraft and was knocked out. Unconscious and unable to use his parachute, he plunged to his death. A short time later his body was recovered from Gade Tower, Hemel Hempstead in Hertfordshire, where it had landed, together with his unopened parachute. As for the Liberator, control was regained and a landing made at nearby RAF Bovingdon.

On the following night, 21 January, an aircraft was lost together with two men. Lt Ferguson was returning from a mission and due west of his last target, when his No 1 engine went off-tune. He was unable to feather it and because it started to vibrate severely, he put the aircraft into a glide to keep up the airspeed. At 12,000ft his No 3 engine started surging and then began to 'run-away'. No 1 started to smoke and, as though it was feeling left out, No 2 began to give trouble. Ferguson had no option but to shut off the fuel to both engines and give the 'bale-out' order. With the exception of Ferguson and Lt Rush his co-pilot, the rest of the crew jumped. As they did, No 3 engine went out. This left just No 4, but that was now whistling. Within seconds the aircraft caught fire and plummeted to earth, exploding on contact with the ground. Both Ferguson and Rush were killed. The radio operator, Russell Onderdonk, broke his leg and before long the rest of the crew joined him in Rheims Hospital with ankle and knee injuries.

Master of Fate

To know where he is, where he is going, and where he has been were three facts a navigator was required to know the answer to at all times. His crew status also required that he worked a longer day, due to the fact that his pre-mission preparation started long before that of his fellow crew members. What was a typical day and sortie like for the 'brains of the crew'? **Howard Bacon** who was a navigator in the Night Leaflet Squadron, recalls:

Above:
Lts Marty Marshall and Art Green from Detachment 113, 18th Weather Squadron.
A. Gulliver/113 Association

Left:
Maj Aber presents the Air Medal to air gunner Jake Sandoval.
J. Sandoval/113 Association

'I don't think you can class any sortie as typical, due to the variability of the targets and the differences in the material we had to deliver, which was diverse in nature. Only our crew remained fairly constant, for which I was eternally grateful. This was because of their vigilance and dedication to all their assigned duties.'

Howard's B-17F, 838, was named *Paper Doll* and coded JJ-O. Some five days after his crew were assigned to it, *Paper Doll* was given some appropriate nose art in the form of a doll, and embellished with the Christian names of his fellow crew members' wives and girlfriends on the engine cowlings. Howard remembers leaflet mission briefings as follows:

'I would get out of my bunk at about 11.00hr, just in time for my lunch at 12.00. Our crew meetings were scheduled for 13.30, at which time the crews going would be selected for the mission. After which, they would be dismissed with the exception of us navigators who were then held for the briefing, and pre-mission preparation.

'Unlike crews in other Bomb Squadrons who flew in mass formations, we in the Night Leaflet Squadron flew alone, and therefore each navigator had his own plans to make up and his own route to plot. So, the responsibility for the accuracy of the mission was squarely in his hands. Instead of making this tougher for us, it actually made it easier in my case, for I felt that I was the "master of my fate" and also of that of my crew, and therefore had to give the best I could. At the briefing I was given flak areas, German fighter airfields, other information that would help me avoid enemy problems, and IFF (Identification Friend or Foe) codes. The entry and re-entry point for the English coast, so that RAF night-fighters would know where and when we would cross the coast (this was to prevent the Germans from sneaking in undetected). Then we were given the most important bit — the targets we were to hit with our leaflet bombs. We were given more than one target per mission, so as to expand the capabilities of reaching more and more people all the time. Last but not least we were given a complete meteorological briefing.'

The 18th Weather Squadron had detachments at every 8th AF base in the British Isles. **Art Gulliver** was assigned to Detachment 113 at Cheddington and, as Leaflet Weather Officer, he recalls:

'We would first give each crew a set of weather maps. These showed the fronts, pressure centres, the precipitation areas along the mission route, and both top and bottom heights of the cloud-base. Also, the expected take-off and landing weather. Attached to the maps was a summary of the conditions, which explained any storms and their direction of movement. A second map was then issued, which showed any high winds and all areas of icing. These areas had their top and bottom heights marked. At all other bomber bases, a horizontal cross-section map was provided for the route. This was not practical at Cheddington however, as each aircraft usually had its own route. Once the maps had been issued, we would brief the crews from a larger map, explaining the expected conditions and stress the hazards, then answer any questions. You could expect the main concern to be the landing conditions when the crews got back — or IF they could expect to get back! We would then explain which airfields were alternatives and the expected conditions there. Crews were also interested in good weather areas over the Continent, as these could be areas where the enemy could sight them from the ground.

'On return from all missions, crews were de-briefed by the same Weather Officer who had briefed them. They would be asked for the conditions that they had experienced on their mission, and which they should have noted on their maps at the time. On completion of the de-brief, we would then return to our office in the control tower, and phone Headquarters 8th AF Bomber Command at High Wycombe. These notes were of the utmost importance to the Weather Officers there, as they would be preparing forecasts for all 8th AF bomber missions which would follow in four to eight hours after the Cheddington aircraft had landed.'

Once the weather briefing was over, it was time to get on with the preparation. **Howard Bacon** continues:

'One of my longest sorties had targets in France at Rennes, Tours, Orleans, and Mulhouse — which was in Eastern France very near to Basle in Switzerland. Armed with all my navaids I plotted the course around any possible trouble areas. On the map it would end up looking great, and I would hope that the flight would go the same way. The exit out of England was Portland Bill which was not a time problem, but as it was also the re-entry point, this did present a problem. It was here that I built in a safety factor, in case of weather changes and in that area there were many. To overcome them, on the way back I would mark a triangle on the map by plotting a heading for a point other than Portland Bill, and then figure out the time at that point for our re-entry time. Then, if we were early we could go further out on the triangle, or if we were late we could cut across the triangle to the turning point to save time, then re-enter at the correct time. The final exactness of the weather report would not be known, however, until our actual flight time.

'When I had finished my planning and plotting at 15.00hrs, I returned to our hut with briefcase in hand, confident I had done the best that I could. Despite the excitement of the moment, I maintained a discipline of not telling my fellow crewmen and brother officers what our target destinations were until they were called to briefing themselves. This was not because I did not trust them to keep their mouths shut, but because I didn't trust myself to keep my own mouth shut. The saying "loose lips sink ships" applied for me at Cheddington, as I had experienced Lord Haw Haw giving the time on our mess hall clock at Chelveston during one of his evening radio broadcasts. The clock was wrong — but he was right! I hate to admit it now, but I would be about to burst trying to keep the target locations to myself.

'Tea was at 17.30hrs, which was followed by odds and ends that I found to do until our full briefing at 20.00hrs, when I would go back briefcase in hand. You could feel the electricity in the air when the time came for target assignments, and when it really sunk in where the crews were going, you could feel their excitement. After the briefing we put on our Mae Wests and picked up our parachutes, then off we went to the aircraft. The 406th Squadron dispersal was over on the northeast side of the field, away from that of the 36th.

'Once in the aircraft my equipment had to be checked out, my first concern being the "G" Box radar unit, which provided me with information I couldn't do without. This was an accurate indication of the wind direction and its speed, but I could only get this after we were in flight. The box had such accuracy in England that I could find my location and with it, our limitations for altitude all round the Base, should there be any fog. We could therefore land without crashing into any of the hills. It required special hyperbolic-type maps with lines defined in three colours. These indicated three different radar sources, and were identifiable as different blips on the screen. I would have to get at least two different blips, and where the lines crossed, that was where we were at that instant in time. If I took a series of these "fixes" I had enough to establish the flight line, and from that result could extract the effect of the wind during the flight, and thus the wind direction and speed. For me the big problem was the shortness of the accuracy range, for once across the Channel the accuracy diminished in relation to the distance away from England. From then on it was "dead reckoning" or DR, and hoping that the winds remained constant throughout the mission.

'After all my checks had been completed, the only thing then left for me to do was wait it out and see if we would go. The mission could be scrubbed at any time, and we would then have to stand down. The worst thing about a mission was to be ready, then have the red flare signal fired by Flying Control indicating to the pilot that his mission was off.

'Once our engines were turning over, I made a last-minute check to make sure the blackout curtain between me and the bombardier was safely in place. This was so that no light could leak out. I would also check my oxygen, then after a green light, brakes were released and we were off. The time was 02.00hrs and for me this was the time I felt like a "one-armed paperhanger". It was the critical period when I had to get the winds while we were climbing to reach our mission altitude, with the pilot following the course I had set for him at each turn. I took for granted he would follow this course as accurately as possible, and I know he tried to maintain it. Things looked good for us as the winds given in briefing were coming from the right direction, and we departed Portland Bill on time, and en route for France. Checks were now made from time to time to verify the wind speed and direction. Even though it was night, the rivers and towns were used to identify our track over the ground, and so could give us an accurate computation of the wind speed and direction.

'On this particular mission, we had just crossed the Channel and were over the bay of St Malo. We had all settled down into our basic routines, with the bombardier anticipating the first drop, when I realised something was wrong! We were too early for the crossing and had arrived there much too fast. A sinking feeling then started to creep in, and I wondered what had gone wrong with my computations. Checking with the bombardier, who agreed with me on identification of St Malo, I quickly refigured our wind speed and direction, and came up with a weird answer for our speed over the ground. The wind pushing us in flight — or the wind mass we were flying in — had reached the unheard-of velocity of 125kt and were cruising at 155-160kt. This meant that we were flying through France at a ground speed of some 280kt. This is all very well, but take the flip side of the coin and it meant we would be crawling back home out of France at only 30-35kt!

'Knowing the problem but not the answer, with the assistance of our bombardier I concentrated on checking landmarks to verify our position, and soon was able to reconfirm our way-points with their new arrival time. We raced into France dropping our leaflet bombs on our assigned targets, with the last drop at Mulhouse way ahead of my original eta. Once we had completed the bomb-run, I informed the rest of the crew about the problem so they would understand the situation, and the reason for the long slow haul home. I then kept constant watch on our ground speed and refigured our time to the re-entry point. The old "Radius of Action" triangle technique worked, and we made our re-entry point right on the nose and were soon back home.

'We landed at 05.50hrs in between day take-offs, and reported in for de-briefing and our usual shot of whisky (if you wanted it). We then all sat down at a table for interrogation and then each individual had his own de-brief. I thought the weather man would

turn inside out when I reported the winds we had encountered. I told him the direction was accurate but the speed far exceeded anything I had ever run up against. It was soon 06.30hrs and time for breakfast — real (not powdered) eggs, toast, and cocoa, then into the sack at 07.00hrs for a good day's sleep, or until our next briefing.'

Those winds Howard encountered are now fully understood, and are known as jetstreams — high altitude almost horizontal winds exceeding 80kt found at the boundary of warm and cold air currents. For Howard it was just another mission, another to help make his final total of 45. Despite being witness to take-off crashes, despite seeing one aircraft shot up so badly that it had to be scrapped, and despite seeing one return with three dead and six wounded on board, what kept him going? He claims to have had a good crew, a first class pilot, a tremendous crew chief who, with his men, always worked above and beyond the call of duty. And that whilst he sat on his 'flak flap', Lady Luck sat on his shoulder.

The Bomb

When leaflet missions first started in 1943, the method of dissemination in bundles with barometric releases was acceptable. That is until their failure was brought to light by a Col Wallace from VIII Bomber Command, who stated:

'We are not getting satisfactory results from the aneroids we are using on our leaflet bundles. The slipstream causes the bundles to

Below and below right:
One of many booklets that gave the man in the street instructions on how to delay or destroy the German war machine. WG2F had 32 pages in both French and German. It was disseminated from 5 September to 28 October 1944.

NACHRICHTEN FÜR DIE TRUPPE

Das mit schweren Blutopfern erkaufte Bure wieder aufgegeben

Angriffsspitze muss zurück

Ardennen-Nachschub droht zu erliegen

(German newspaper article text)

"Wer Volksopfer bestiehlt, stirbt!"

Von Wedel soll Canaris ersetzen

Russische Pferde ziehen Berliner Droschken

Karlsruher Bahnhöfe durch Bomben zerstört

Schwedens Polizei sucht scheintoten SS-Führer

T. 270

Left:
T270: Nachrichten Fur Die Truppe

Issue 270, the 11 January 1945 copy of 'News For The Troops'. It was the first Allied daily newspaper for German troops, and reported up-to-date war-news, sports results and even displayed pin-ups! *Nachricten* was disseminated from 25 April 1944 to Issue 381 on 7 May 1945.

open up directly below the aircraft, which means that leaflets destined for Paris end up in North Africa or Turkey. Either this or the leaflets go all the way down in a bundle. Will you see what you can do on this?'

His statement was no exaggeration of the situation, for week after week errors became the norm. On one of the first leaflet missions, aircraft of the 422nd Squadron had to drop leaflets destined for the Paris area over Brussels! This was just to combat the prevailing 60mph winds that were present at 30,000ft. As for the problem of the leaflets falling intact as a bundle, *The Manchester Guardian* reported that 'one fell solidly on to a small German barge, went through the bottom, and sunk it. Another bundle crashed through the roof of Notre Dame Cathedral . . .'!

A new problem was highlighted when VIII Bomber Command changed the strategy of its bombardment campaign from explosive, to the devastating effect of incendiary bombs on German urban areas. Little did anyone think it would change leaflet operations or policy, but it became increasingly evident that, due to the number of internal aircraft fires being started by the pre-ignition of bomb fuses, the mixture of incendiary bombs being transported along with leaflets added a new hazard to bombing missions. Leaflets could be loaded in bomb-bays with 500 and 2,000lb bombs, but would not mix with clusters of incendiaries. Crews were also faced with, and complained of, the additional drag that was being caused by the extra weight of up to

Gibt es wirklich keine Brücken mehr . . . .

zwischen dem deutschen Volk und der freien Welt?

Die Antwort auf diese Frage bestimmt in diesen Stunden das Handeln oder Nichthandeln aller deutschen Menschen. Von dieser Antwort hängt DEINE Zukunft ab!

Goebbels sagt: „Das deutsche Volk hat alle Brücken hinter sich abgebrochen . . ."

Für Goebbels, Hitler, Himmler und Co. ist das kein Problem. Für die besessenen Fanatiker und zum Untergang verurteilten Führer der deutschen Tragödie gibt es in der Tat keine Brücke. Weder eine Brücke zur europäischen Zivilisation — noch zu einer besseren deutschen Zukunft.

Für die Partei und SS-Fanatiker gibt es nur den UNTERGANG.

UN APPEL AUX TRAVAILLEURS FRANCAIS ET BELGES EN ALLEMAGNE

L'Allemagne a perdu la guerre ! La fin de la plus grande guerre de l'histoire approche — mais. . . .

VOUS ETES EN DANGER !

A mesure que la guerre tire à sa fin le régime nazi deviendra de plus en plus impitoyable. Chacun de vous dorénavant est sous le coup d'UN DOUBLE DANGER. Le DANGER émanant des terroristes nazis qui, pour obtenir le maximum de rendement de votre part, useront contre vous de tous les moyens. Et le DANGER — chaque jour plus grand — des ATTAQUES AERIENNES.

Vous serez contraints à vivre et à travailler dans les régions qui renferment les plus dangereux des objectifs choisis par les Forces Aériennes Alliées — tandis que les adolescents allemands de seize ans et les vieillards de soixante ans et de plus seront dirigés vers le front pour servir de dernières réserves de chair à canon dans les batailles de Hitler acculé. Ne dites pas: Nous savons ce que sont les bombardements.

VOUS N'AVEZ ENCORE RIEN VU.

Vous serez versés de force dans l'armée allemande pour combler les rangs ravagés de la Wehrmacht vaincue.

800lb of leaflets. This made it difficult for the captain in each of the three B-17s in the tail-end position to keep up, and as a result they lost the protection of the large box formations of bombers.

At the same time as the crews were having misgivings on mixing bomb-loads, engineering officers at American bomber bases were beginning to think that the additional weight of the leaflets (now being transported in heavy canvas bags) might cause the aircraft to buckle during violent, evasive action from fighters or flak. The bags had replaced the wooden boxes and were strapped to the main longerons of the aircraft. When the last bomb was released, it jerked open the neck of the bag which had been kept closed by wire, thus allowing the leaflets to fall out.

A solution to the airframe distortion possibility was submitted by Lt Bloomer, a junior engineering officer in VIII Bomber Command. He suggested loading bundles of leaflets into many large wooden boxes rather than just one, but using only ONE aircraft. This aircraft could then carry 3,500lb of leaflets in each of the large slatted boxes. Thus, each aircraft alone could carry more than the 24,000lb that were being carried by three aircraft using the bags, but still keep the aircraft light for manoeuvring. This method was accepted and put into practice.

Despite the changes and improvements in the equipment, and the increase in volume of leaflets now being disseminated, the British PWE reported that an average of only 4% of leaflets dropped were finding their way into the hands of the enemy. What was needed was a device that would allow accurate dissemination over the required target area. The idea of using a readily available device that was present on the airfield at Chelveston came first to the 305th Bomb Group Operations Officer, Capt James Monroe. He investigated some old laminated paper containers that had housed M-17 incendiary bombs. They were 48in long, had a diameter of 16½in, and were light but strong with the ends enclosed by cardboard caps. Furthermore, they were NOT needed. Capt Monroe, with foresight, saw they had potential. With the addition of just a pair of standard

General Eisenhower taler til de besatte Lande i Europa

VESTEUROPAS FOLK!

Troppestyrker fra de Allieredes Ekspeditionshær er gaaet i Land paa den franske Kyst. Denne Landgang er et Led i de forenede Nationers fælles Plan, som er lagt sammen med vo'r store, russiske Allierede, og som tager Sigte paa at befri Europa.

Jeg bringer Dem alle dette Budskab. Selv om det indledende Angreb maaske ikke er blevet foretaget i Deres eget Land, er Befrielsens Time dog nær.

Alle Patrioter, Mænd og Kvinder, Unge og Gamle, har en Indsats at gøre, naar den endelige Sejr skal vindes. Til Medlemmerne af Modstandsbevægelserne, hvadenten de faar deres Ordrer hjemmefra eller udefra, siger jeg : " Følg de Instruktioner, De har faaet." Til Patrioter, som ikke tilhører organiserede Modstandsgrupper, siger jeg : " Udsæt ikke Deres Liv for unødig Fare, men fortsæt Deres passive Modstand, indtil jeg giver Dem Signalet til Rejsning og til Angreb paa Fjenden. Den Dag vil komme, hvor jeg faar Brug for Deres samlede Styrke." Indtil den Dag paalægger jeg Dem den haarde Opgave at udvise Disciplin og Tilbageholdenhed.

FRANKRIGS BORGERE!

Jeg er stolt over atter at have Frankrigs tapre Styrker under min Kommando. I Kampen ved deres Allieredes Side vil de spille en fortjenstfuld Rolle under deres Fædrelands Befrielse.

Fordi den første Landgang har fundet Sted paa Deres Lands Jord, gentager jeg over for Dem med endnu større Eftertryk mit Budskab til Befolkningerne i de andre besatte Lande i Vesteuropa. Følg Deres Lederes Instruktioner. En forhastet Rejsning af alle Franskmænd kan komme til at forhindre Dem i at yde Deres Land den størst mulige Hjælp i det kritiske Øjeblik. Vær taalmodige og hold Dem beredt !

Som Øverstkommanderende for de Allieredes Ekspeditionshær er det min Pligt og mit Ansvar at træffe alle nødvendige Forholdsregler i Forbindelse med Krigsførelsen. Det er af største Betydning, at de Ordrer, jeg udsteder, bliver efterkommet hurtigt og villigt.

En effektiv fransk Civiladministration maa foretages af Franskmænd. Enhver maa fortsætte sit nuværende Arbejde, medmindre han modtager andre Ordrer. De, som har gjort fælles Sag med Fjenden og saaledes forraadt deres Land, vil blive fjernet. Naar Frankrig er blevet befriet for Undertrykkerne, maa det franske Folk selv vælge sine Repræsentanter og den Regering, det ønsker at leve under.

Under dette Felttog, hvis Maal er Fjendens endelige Nederlag, vil De maaske lide yderligere Tab eller Skade. Hvor tragisk dette end er, er det en Del af den Pris, der maa betales for Sejren. Jeg forsikrer Dem om, at jeg vil gøre alt, hvad der staar i min Magt, for at lette Deres Prøvelser. Jeg ved, at jeg nu i lige saa høj Grad som tidligere kan regne med Deres faste Holdning. Den tapre Indsats, der er blevet gjort af de Franskmænd, som baade i selve Frankrig og overalt i det franske Imperium har fortsat Kampen mod Nazisterne og deres Lejesvende i Vichy, har været et Eksempel og en Inspiration for os alle.

Denne Landgang er blot den indledende Fase af Felttoget i Vesteuropa. Der ligger store Slag foran os. Jeg opfordrer alle frihedselskende Mennesker til at slutte sig til os. Vær tillidsfulde og standhaftige ; — vore Stridskræfter er resolutte ; — sammen vil vi vinde Sejr.

DWIGHT D. EISENHOWER.
Øverstkommanderende for de
Allieredes Ekspeditionshær

AUX HABITANTS DES ZONES DE COMBAT

AVIS DU COMMANDEMENT SUPREME ALLIE

RAIDS AERIENS—VOTRE VILLE PEUT ETRE UN OBJECTIF !

Même s'il n'y a pas actuellement de troupes allemandes dans votre région, il peut se trouver dans votre ville des ponts, des viaducs, des installations ferroviaires, des réservoirs de carburant, des usines, des ateliers de réparations, etc. . . . qui pourront être à un moment donné d'importance vitale pour l'ennemi, au cours de sa retraite de France.

L'attaque de ces installations par les forces aériennes alliées peut faire partie des opérations de la libération. Il ne sera pas toujours possible de vous avertir à l'avance de ces attaques. En conséquence :

1. Dites-vous toujours que l'apparition de bombardiers alliés peut signifier que des troupes allemandes ou des installations vitales de votre ville sont sur le point d'être attaquées.

2. Si vous en avez le moyen, quittez la ville. Si vous devez rester là, ne traînez pas dans les rues ou sur les ponts ; réfugiez-vous dans les abris, dans des caves profondes, ou au rez-de-chaussée de votre maison, sous l'escalier ; couchez-vous par terre, écartez-vous des verres.

AVANT QUE LA BATAILLE APPROCHE

Soyez prêts à quitter la ville au premier avertissement. Les armées de la libération se déplacent rapidement.

1. Préservez vos biens de l'ennemi, y compris les vêtements civils.

2. Ayez toujours prête une réserve de nourriture et d'eau, suffisante pour plusieurs jours, et dissimulez-la à l'ennemi.

3. Construisez une tranchée ou un abri dans la campagne, aussi près que possible de chez vous, mais assez loin des routes, des chemins de fer, des ponts, et autres objectifs militaires.

4. Que votre tranchée ou votre abri soit assez large pour recevoir votre famille et assez profonde pour vous permettre de vous coucher par terre. Couvrez-la avec de branches et du gazon.

ZWEI WORTE die 1 600 000 Leben retteten

„EI SÖRRENDER" sagten allein im Westen 1 600 000 Deiner Kameraden, weil sie einsahen, dass ihre Lage hoffnungslos war.

„EI SÖRRENDER" bedeutete für 1 600 000 Deiner Kameraden, dass sie aus der Hölle der Materialschlacht in Sicherheit gelangten.

„EI SÖRRENDER" bedeutete für 1 600 000 Deiner Kameraden, dass sie die Heimat nach Kriegsende gesund und wohlbehalten wiedersehen.

Auch für Dich öffnen ZWEI WORTE den Weg in die Heimat. ZWEI WORTE:

„EI SÖRRENDER"

Above:
ZF10 People of Combat Zones
Disseminated over France from 14 August up to and including 19 November 1944. It advised all local civilians to keep clear of roads, bridges and railways.

Right:
ZG126: I Surrender
One of a number of leaflets that were directed at German troops. It pointed out some facts on who had surrendered, and advised them to do the same. It was disseminated on the nights of 13 to 17 April 1944.

56

'U-bolts', they could be attached to the normal issue bomb shackles. The containers, when full of leaflets, could then be hung in the bomb-bays of B-17 Flying Fortress aircraft. All he now needed was to find out if they would be stable in flight and if they could be made to open at a desired height for the contents to empty and cover the nominated target area.

Working in one of the 305th's hangars, he conducted research into the fitting of standard M-111 bomb time-fuses into the end of the containers. Then after drilling down both sides, he fed primer cord through the ½in diameter holes that were spaced at 6in intervals. The cord was terminated next to the explosive fuse, which was sunk into a length of pipe so as to increase the explosive effect of the detonation. When assembled, Monroe took the completed bomb outside the hangar, then, after detonation of the nose fuse, saw that the container had been blown apart! All that was now required was some drawings of the device so that additional 'Monroe T-1 Bombs' could be made and then test-flown. The first test was held on 21 January 1944, when a T-1 was loaded into a B-17 flown by Capt Hitchcock. Also on board as an observer was Gen Robert McClure, Chief of the PWD section of the Supreme Headquarters Allied Expeditionary Forces (SHAEF), with which Monroe had just been placed on Detached Service. Monroe was on board an observation plane flown by Maj Aber and Capt August Weil (Weil had just replaced Monroe as the new Operations Officer). Aber's crew also included Jake Sandoval the tail gunner, who recalls the test and claims, 'I saw nothing'.

The intended height of the test was to have been 5,000ft, with split-second timing. To achieve this, radio contact was to have been established on the frequency used as the 305th Command Frequency, but at the time of the test it was being used for a mission! The two aircraft were thus unable to communicate, and in manoeuvring to the test area over the North Sea, missed each other. All Aber could do now was to put on a second test when there was a lull in missions, and if the weather permitted. The chance came on 4 February, when the Fortress dropped the test bomb from 10,000ft. A total weight of 300lb of paper had been packed in the bomb, most in the fuse end to make it stable in fall, and Jake's observation aircraft with Monroe and camera on board flew at 6,000ft. Also on board were Allan Challas who was head of the Office of War Information (OWI), Sam Boal, of the London OWI, Maj Robert Garey, Liaison Officer at HQ 8th AF, and Sqn Ldr Peter Branch RAF, SHAEF. A free radio frequency had been obtained and allowed contact to be maintained between the two aircraft. As a result, at 15.00hrs and on a Gee signal, the bomb fell free from the bomb-bay, rolled twice, then — when at 1,000ft below the Fortress — detonated. The paper contents showed good dispersal and began to separate into single sheets with the bomb disintegrating into harmless bits. As a result of the test, a report was submitted three days later by Maj Aber and Capt Monroe to the 305th Headquarters, detailing the events and reporting the fact that leaflet bombs could now be brought down to explode from 30,000ft to 2,000ft, and target an area as small as a half to one mile, or as large as required.

The first operational use of the Monroe bomb was on 18 April 1944, when the 422nd added a new location for squadron operations — Norway. The intention was for five B-17s to drop 2,560,000 copies of leaflet N4 entitled 'Come it Will' over the Stavanger, Oslo, Bergen and Trondheim area. With Aber's crew

Passierschein

Der deutsche Soldat, der diesen Passierschein vorzeigt, benutzt ihn als Zeichen seines ehrlichen Willens, sich zu ergeben. Er ist zu entwaffnen. Er muß gut behandelt werden. Er hat Anspruch auf Verpflegung und, wenn nötig, ärztliche Behandlung. Er wird so bald wie möglich aus der Gefahrenzone entfernt.

Dwight Eisenhower
OBERBEFEHLSHABER
der alliierten Expeditions-Armeen

Englische Übersetzung nachstehend. Sie dient als Anweisung an die alliierten Vorposten.

SAFE CONDUCT

The German soldier who carries this safe conduct is using it as a sign of his genuine wish to give himself up. He is to be disarmed, to be well looked after, to receive food and medical attention as required, and to be removed from the danger zone as soon as possible.

Dwight Eisenhower
SUPREME COMMANDER,
Allied Expeditionary Force

DAS ENDE EINER DIVISION

Überlebende der 716. I.D. (Kreml-Division) sind jetzt in Sicherheit in England. Ihre Berichte sind EINE WARNUNG FÜR ALLE TRUPPEN AM ATLANTIKWALL — DIE AUF ENTSATZ WARTEN

Hier ist einer der Berichte :

„Am Dienstag war der erste Angriff auf unseren Abschnitt zwischen Arromanches und Ouistreham. Da kriegten wir gleich den Befehl : Aushalten — Verstärkung im Anmarsch !

Am Donnerstag waren wir praktisch schon überrannt und eingekesselt. Rückwärts war der Feind mit kanadischen Fallschirmjägern. Vorne lag der Feind mit Schlachtschiffen und zerharkte uns die Stellung. Und über uns da hing der Feind mit einer dicken Fliegerdecke und jagte uns mit Flächenwürfen die letzten Minenfelder hoch.

Kein deutscher Jäger zu sehen. Keine Verbindung mehr mit rechts und links — alles was wir wussten war : der Anglo-Amerikaner landet dauernd Truppen und schweres Material auf beiden Seiten.

Und von Verstärkung keine Rede. Nur wieder der Befehl vom Kommandeur kam durch : Aushalten bis zum letzten Schuss !

Da lagen wir so gut wie nackt in unseren ausgeschlitzten Bunkern und sollten mit unseren Maschinenpistolen und MGs und Pak-Geschützen die Stellung halten bis zum letzten Schuss — und kamen garnicht zum Schuss. Ab und zu hat einer nach den Fliegern geschossen, das war alles.

Am Donnerstag abend hiess es wieder : Es kommt Verstärkung. Wir werden 'rausgehauen. Von Caen sind Panzer unterwegs.

Die Panzer haben wir nie zu sehen gekriegt. Das war nur eine schöne Geste, — mehr nicht. Eine Abteilung von der 21. P.D. mit Panzer IV — mit sowas kamen sie an am dritten

ZG 11

WENN ES LOSGEHT

Heute lebst Du noch. Du kämpfst mit unzureichenden Waffen, mit mangelhafter Ausrüstung, von halbgeschulten Einheiten umgeben. Aber - Du lebst. Tausende Deiner Kameraden, viele Deiner eigenen Freunde sind gefallen. Es war schlimm, aber Du bist noch entkommen. Du lebst. Deine Offiziere verwerfen Deine Gedanken, dass das nur eine Kampfpause ist. Es besteht Hoffnung, denn - Du lebst.

Morgen kann es losgehen wie es auf einmal losging am Atlantikwall bei Avranches und St. Lo. Morgen: Plötzliches, pausenloses Trommelfeuer aller Kaliber, rollender Einsatz von Jabos; tausende von Fliegenden Festungen; Bombenteppiche; Panzer, panzerbrechende Raketenwaffen und die neuen Flammenwerfer. Alles, was Du bisher gesehen hast, war im Vergleich damit ein Kinderspiel. Morgen: Die Hölle.

Übermorgen wird es aus sein und Du bist entweder tot, ein Krüppel oder Kriegsgefangener. Die Entscheidung darüber liegt vielleicht an Dir selbst. Deshalb bedenke jetzt was Du machen wirst wenn Du noch am Leben bist wenn die Materialschlacht über Dich hinwegrollt. Dann ist vielleicht für Dich Gelegenheit, Dein Leben zu retten. Viele werden sich ergeben müssen. Somancher wird aber sterben müssen weil er die Wahl zu spät getroffen hat.

WELCHE WAHL TRIFFST DU ?

Above left:
ZG61: Safe Conduct
The very successful 'safe conduct pass'. Disseminated from 10 September 1944 to 8 March 1945. Over 70% of prisoners of war had these with them when they surrendered.

Above:
ZG11: A Division Written Off
Another tactical leaflet aimed at the German soldier, informing him of the loss of a unit. It was disseminated from 15 June to 14 August 1944. There were a total of 95 tactical leaflets produced in the 'ZG' series.

Left:
ZG82K: What Is To Be Done?
Disseminated from 13 November 1944 to 8 March 1945.

in the lead aircraft, the 10hr mission — with 'Tokyo Tanks' to carry the extra fuel — went as planned, but as a leaflet drop at night it was unsuccessful. Norwegian reports which arrived in London afterwards said that whilst leaflets had been spotted and picked up in fairly large quantities at a small town southeast of Oslo, only three of the other target areas had seen them, and near Bergen and Trondheim the leaflets had burst over a fjord. Also, many leaflets had landed in too high a concentration and could therefore be easily and quickly picked up by German troops. Monroe's explanation in a report to SHAEF was that the M-111 fuses had been set for too low an altitude and had exploded at only 20 to 25ft. The wind therefore was unable to disseminate them. He stated it would not happen again, as issue of the M-111 fuse had dried up and the British Type 860 barometric fuse would be utilised on all future missions. This fuse was set to detonate at 2,000ft, was available in large numbers, and had proved to be more reliable when fitted to parachute flares.

LE COURRIER DE L'AIR

APPORTE PAR AVION   *LONDRES, LE 5 JUILLET 1944.*

Dans Cherbourg libérée

QUATRE PAGES DE PHOTOGRAPHIES

Le 27 juin 1944, les forces américaines commandées par le major-général Collins, faisaient leur entrée dans Cherbourg.

A l'exception de quelques forts, les Allemands, commandés par le lieutenant-général Carl von Schlieben, mettaient bas les armes.

Ainsi s'est terminée la deuxième phase du débarquement allié sur le sol normand; la libération de Cherbourg, première grande ville française à être affranchie du joug allemand, offre aux Alliés une base dont toute l'importance se fera sentir dès que les travaux de réaménagement du port seront terminés.

L'expérience acquise en Afrique du Nord permet de croire qu'ils seront rapidement achevés.

La libération de Cherbourg constitue le point final d'une brillante manœuvre des troupes américaines.

Brièvement, la bataille s'est déroulée comme suit :

Les Américains ont d'abord coupé, sur un front étroit, la base du Cotentin entre Carentan et Barneville.

Contrairement aux prévisions du Haut Commandement allié les Allemands ne réussirent pas à contre-attaquer utilement l'enclave américaine, ni au nord ni au sud.

Au nord, une seule contre-attaque fut lan-cée mais elle fut brisée par l'artillerie.

Au sud où, sur la carte la situation était éminemment favorable à une manœuvre décisive de la part de Rommel, rien de tel ne fut tenté.

Pour comprendre cette carence de Rommel, il faut examiner quelle était, au moment où les Américains ont lancé l'assaut de Cherbourg, la situation dans le secteur britannique entre Caumont et Caen.

Les puissantes formations de blindés mises en action par le général Montgomery au sud-est de la tête de pont alliée y avaient fixé quatre divisions blindées allemandes dans une bataille statique et défensive.

Rommel, durement pressé, sachant qu'une rupture de son front dans ce secteur aurait des conséquences incalculables, fut contraint de choisir de deux maux le moindre.

Assignant à la majeure partie de ses blindés disponibles un rôle d'arrêt entre Caen et Caumont, il n'a pu gêner sérieusement le déploiement américain dans le Cotentin.

M. Stimson, Ministre américain de la Guerre, rendant hommage aux troupes britanniques, a déclaré que la victoire américaine dans le Cotentin était due en grande partie aux opérations menées par les Britanniques et les Canadiens dans le secteur Caumont-Caen.

Le drapeau blanc remplace la croix gammée. Le général von Schlieben sort de son P.C. souterrain

Von Schlieben arrive au Quartier Général du major-général Collins

Left:
F73: Le Courrier De L'Air
The 5 July 1944 issue of *Courier*, disseminated from 10 July to 7 August 1944. It was a four-page French newspaper which preceded *L'Amerique en Guerre*. Very pictorial and with the latest war news for the French people.

As for bomb manufacture, the men at Chelveston constructed the first few Monroe bombs, but as the requirement for more arose, a detachment of an Army Ammunition Company at nearby Sharnbrook in Bedfordshire took over the production. In a short time, and due to a report claiming that the Sharnbrook personnel handled the explosive components in a dangerous way, production was changed to the 8th AF Ordnance Depot at Melchbourne Park. The first Monroe bombs manufactured there came off the production line on 16 May 1944, and by D-Day there were some 4,000 bombs ready. By the end of 1944, a total of 75,277 had been produced — some with assistance of a civilian contractor — and from this total 6,000 were for shipment overseas. Both the T-1 and latter versions of the bomb that had fins and a Type 860 fuse, known as the 'T-2', turned haphazard leaflet bombing missions into an accurate and essential operation.

To keep pace with the Monroe bomb that could not only disseminate leaflets better, but hold more, the production of leaflets had to be quickened. The Luton-based printers Home Counties Newspapers, who owned and published the *Luton News* and many other local newspapers, can take much of the credit — if not all — and were engaged on important war-related leaflet printing work from the onset of war in 1939. Their original leaflet commission, from the Political Intelligence Department (PID) of the Foreign Office, was for half-tone and line blocks of print. To complete this order long hours of work were required which included daily collection of the print blocks by car from nearby Woburn Abbey, from where many famous journalists had been conscripted to write the copy. The success of the operation so impressed the PID that, in 1940, it requested a new weekly production — *Courier de L'Air*. The *Courier* which was a 'White' propaganda newspaper in French, was produced by gravure at other printers, but the typesetting contract was given to the *Luton News* and resulted in the work being completed during the evenings. The text was set at four times its finished size then the proofs reduced photographically. Before long, staff were setting papers in five languages and working two evening shifts to comply with the mandate.

In 1944 the staff of the *Luton News* produced what became one of the finest achievements for the provincial press. Early in March a contract was issued to produce the first daily newspaper for German troops, *Nachrichten für die Truppe*. The idea was to give enemy troops the real truth about the military and general situation on both war and home fronts. In April the PID provided a test issue of two pages measuring 13in × 9in in size, for the *Luton News* to print. Arrangements were made to cut the paper at the associate firm of Leagrave Press, which was also based in Luton. On 25 April the first issue was printed, and after being tied up in convenient bales on the publishing bench, was transported the 2½ miles to the Leagrave Press, 'knocked up' by female labour then put through two guillotines, the first of which cut off the fold, the second dividing the two copies. They were then loaded into leaflet bombs and transported by men of the NLS to the airfield to be flown out that night.

Production of *Nachrichten* continued up to 6 June 1944, 'The Big Day', when process staff came in at 03.30hrs. By 10.00hrs they were running the greatest war story ever to roll off local or national presses, official, and with full details. The staff who until then had been locked in the factory, had been unable to say a word to anyone outside their building!

From the initial edition of 200,000 single-sheet copies, production rose to 1,000,000 on D-Day. The print run was then set at 800,000 copies of a four-page newspaper, seven days a week. As the Allied advance approached the River Rhine in early 1945, the daily order was increased to 1,000,000 again and carried on at this figure until the German surrender in May.

To put on record the thanks of the Political Intelligence Department, its Chief, **Harold Keeble**, sent the following letter to John Gibbs of the *Luton News* on 8 April 1945:

'Now that your Presses have turned out the last issue of *Nachrichten*, I should like you to know how much I personally appreciate the great work which you and your staff have put in on this paper.

'I hope it is some satisfaction to you all to have launched the world's first airborne daily newspaper. I hope, too, that the splendid enthusiasm which you have shown in the production of the *Nachrichten* will be echoed in our new enterprise which starts on Tuesday.

'This new paper — which is to be called *SHAEF*, with the subtitle *The Official Organ of the Supreme Allied Command*, also breaks new ground in publishing history. It is the first time a Supreme Commander has been able to sponsor a venture of this kind and Gen Eisenhower believes that its development will have an important part to play during the period of chaos and collapse.

'Again, my warmest thanks to you all'.

One way of assessing the effect leaflets had on the enemy was by interrogation of prisoners of war. *'Leaflet Reactions'*, — a notice issued by SHAEF at regular periods, reported the results of these interrogations and also gave the latest news on PsyWar Operations. The following examples display its style and content.

'Out of a sample group of 200 prisoners captured in and around Aachen in the middle of October, approximately 50% had leaflets on their person at the time of their capture.'
'An interesting commentary on the value attached to our Safe Conduct Leaflet ZG61 by the German soldier comes in a report from the Third Army. They have received information from

prisoners that Allied 'Safe Conduct Leaflets' have a high trading value for cigarettes and other items in special demand within the German lines.'

'A report from the 21st Army Group says that almost all prisoners taken along their sector of the front prove to have had some contact with our leaflets. One was particularly impressed by a leaflet describing the conditions in prisoner-of-war camps.'

'The Peoples Court of Innsbruck has passed a sentence of death on Joseph Axinger for "the offence of picking up and distributing dropped leaflets".'

'Out of a sample group of 69 prisoners taken at Lorient, 29 stated that Allied leaflets had influenced their decision to give themselves up. 70% of the group reported that they had seen Allied leaflets; of these 50% were familiar with the Safe Conduct Pass. 40% recalled one or more of the following: *Nachrichten* (T series), *You Are Surrounded* (ZG38), *How Your Comrades Fared* (ZG54), *Polish Language Leaflet* (ZG10) and the special *Lorient* leaflet (ZG47).'

The back of the *Counter Attack* leaflet (ZG77) carries a 'five Minute Blitz Course for German G.I.s' consisting of German-English translations for a number of key phrases. 1st Army reports the course seems to be getting results. Many have come over, leaflet in hand, shouting the words 'I surrender'.

'A Prusso-Phobe Bavarian read the PWB leaflet containing the text of the Aachen ultimatum. He decided to desert, took a Viennese comrade along, and persuaded eleven others to join. They marched to the US lines waving the leaflets and white flags.'

'The Commanding Officer of the 2nd Battalion, 1215 Grenadiers, 462 German Infantry, has given his troops a strong warning to those who find Allied leaflets to turn them in UNREAD.'
'A group of fighters were used for the first time in this theatre to carry the psychological warfare campaign to the enemy. Instead of bombs, Thunderbolts dropped leaflet ZG34 (*German Generals Proclaim Peace Government*) near Chartres and between St Quentin and Compiegne. 31 July.'

' "Clumping" by leaflets in bundles will now be avoided by the use of leaflets bombs. Dissemination of *Arc en Ciel* over Belgium for July (XB18, XB19, XB20, XB21) amounted to 1,544,000 copies.'

'You will be interested to hear that when the final count came in for Le Havre it showed 11,302 prisoners out of a garrison of 12,000. Analysis show that over 75% had leaflets on them.'
'Korvetten Kapitän Fritz Otto, now a prisoner, informed us that with leaflets falling all around his troops he found himself leading a "bunch of neurotics" and gave the whole thing up — coming over to us ... Thanks again for the great assistance, and please pass on my thanks to the gang who are actually doing the dropping. They are doing a great job and it is really being appreciated.'

Life in the Squadron

Life for an officer or enlisted man in the NLS was far from dull. If there were no missions to be flown, there was training, and if there was no training, there were always the rules and squadron policies to be adhered to. Col Aber implemented these rules not to confuse, heckle, or depress his staff, but to let them know exactly what he required of each and every one of them so they could all help their squadron accomplish its mission. All new members of the squadron were acquainted with the following rules and procedures, as soon as they arrived for duty with the NLS at Cheddington:

Formations

New crews had to have formation meetings every day at 09.00 and 13.30hrs, that were held on the Instructional Site. Once combat training had been completed and the crew operational, only one formation meeting had to be attended each day. This was held at 13.30hrs in the Briefing Room. All crews, both officers and enlisted men, had to be present and attendance lists were taken to ensure this was complied with.

Passes

The men were expected to 'work like hell' while on duty at the Base, but when off duty their time was their own to do with what they liked, provided of course it was within 'Theatre Regulations'. New crews could expect their first pass to be issued after being on Base for two weeks and after having their security lecture. After that a crew could expect to go off the Base 'on Pass' every two to three weeks. Passes were granted by operations in co-ordination with the Orderly Room. They began at 12.00hrs, and terminated 48hr later. The Pass Roster was kept in Operations so the First Pilot could ascertain when his crew would be off the Base. The 13.30hrs Formation Meeting held the day the Pass started could be missed, but it had to be attended on the day of return to the Base. All officers had to sign-out in the register that was kept in Operations, when leaving the Base and likewise on return to the Base. It had to be signed personally, and in addition, one of the 'Duty' Operations Officers had to be informed. There were only two cases when this was not necessary: for absence of less than two hours from the Base, or when going on the 'Liberty Run'. These runs consisted of several buses that left the Base gym every night at 19.00hrs for the American Red Cross Club in Luton, and returned to the Base at 23.00hrs. For enlisted men, green Class 'B' passes were available for off-duty hours and were good within a 25-mile radius of the Base. They expired at 01.00hrs and had to be returned after being used.

Bulletin Boards

Any official squadron or command notice was displayed on two notice boards. One located in Site 3 and the other in the Operations Building. Each officer had to read and initial them daily, for Aber claimed 'an officer who reads the notice board knows what's going on in his squadron'.

Uniforms

The only item of flying equipment that could be worn off the flying line was the now-famous 'A-2' leather jacket. It could be worn around the Base, but never in the Mess or Officers' Club. For the evening meal either the blouse or battle jacket was acceptable but, if flying a mission that night or having flown that afternoon and the crew member did not have time to go to his quarters and change, he could wear his Class 'B' uniform. For all formal occasions including the squadron dances that were held each month, the blouse had to be worn. When off the Base either the blouse or battle jacket was acceptable, as well as the well known 'crusher' hat. Whilst cycling it was not necessary to wear either the jacket or blouse, but one had to carry one or the other and wear one's cap. Officers were allowed to wear GI shoes, but not the rough-finished type. They had, however, to be kept very well polished. White socks were forbidden, only tan being worn. There were inspections to ensure these conditions were being met and 'dog tags' being worn and, if pullovers were used, that they could not be seen. The only true personal choice was the wearing of 'pinks' — beige trousers with green shirt, or vice versa.

Below:
A number of the airmen made good friends whilst in England and were often taken in and treated as one of the family.
J. Reeve/113 Association

Below right:
Sixty-plus even got married, including the 406th Gunnery Officer Lt Gugenhein. *B. Gunderson/113 Association*

Promotion

Just because an individual was an aircrew member, it was not necessarily a guarantee of promotion. The following standards were considered, however, when selecting officers for promotion to 1st Lieutenants, or Flight Officers to 2nd Lieutenants:

Pilot

He had to complete a sufficient number of operational hours to demonstrate unquestionable proficiency as pilot on the type of aircraft he flew. He had also to demonstrate, both in the air and on the ground, the qualities of a well disciplined officer, and in particular the way he handled his crew and how he discharged his ground duties. When a pilot satisfactorily demonstrated that he possessed the right qualities he was then recommended for 1st Lieutenant. Subsequently, out of the entire group of pilots, the three most outstanding in proficiency, initiative, aggressiveness and 'officer-like' qualities were chosen as Flight Commanders. This position carried the rank of captain, provided the officer continued to measure up to the high standards. He also had to remain with the squadron after his tour of combat had been completed for a period of about one to two months, in order to help with the flight training of replacement crews.

Co-Pilot

He had to complete a minimum of 100 operational hours before assessment as first pilot in the type of aircraft he was assigned to. To enable him to do this his pilot was allowed to give him transition flight training until he considered him to be proficient. The co-pilot would then be given a check ride by the Flight Commander who would look for good aircraft control during take-off, approaches and on landings. He would also expect a good circuit to be flown and see a good mastery of all emergency procedures. If found acceptable, the co-pilot would then be given another check ride, this time by Col Aber, or either his Air Executive or Operations Officer. He would also have to be an efficient officer, both in the air and on the ground.

Navigators

Likewise, he had to be efficient, fly a minimum 100hr on operations and demonstrate a high degree of skill in all types of

Left:
A NLS B-24 that left runway 26 too early! *N. Senter/113 Association*

navigation, in particular DR (dead-reckoning) and the use of the G-Box.

Bombardiers

In the NLS he occupied a peculiar position due to the fact that there was no opportunity for him to demonstrate his proficiency as a Precision Bombardier. Other standards were therefore devised to determine his eligibility for promotion. The Navigation Department conducted a school in DR and G-Box for all bombardiers, which enabled supervisory personnel to make observations on the individual's ability to navigate, his eagerness, initiative, attitude and attention to duty. In addition, the conduct of each bombardier, both on the ground and in the air, was carefully noted. All these observations taken together formed the basis on which bombardiers were recommended for promotion.

Enlisted Men

They had to prove themselves deserving of promotion by being good crew members, and good NCO material. All would be sergeants before flying operationally and subsequently the radio operator and engineer would become a staff sergeant, and the latter a tech sergeant. All gunners became staff sergeants.

Inspections

Enlisted men's barracks were inspected each day by the Flight Commander at 14.15hrs. On Saturdays, at 13.00hrs, the Squadron Commander also inspected them. In addition, he inspected the officers' quarters at the same time.

Tour of Combat and Awards

In accordance with the policy set by HQ 8th AF, the tour of combat for heavy bombardment crews in the latter stages of the war was

Above:
Lt Heusser and his crew along with *Paper Doll*. Standing left to right: Lt Heusser, pilot; Bill Taylor, waist gunner; Rusty Emerick, radio op; Ted Lewis, co-pilot; Herb Bobinger, ball turret. Kneeling: Dean McConn, navigator; Walt Rogells, tail gunner; Ray Sefrna, bombardier; Ed Stearns, flight engineer; Joe Roden, waist gunner.
B. Gunderson/113 Association

Right:
Against the backdrop of a wintry landscape in March 1945, the crew of B-24 *Dark Eyes* pose for the camera. Standing: Eugene Chambers, pilot; Walt Longanecker, co-pilot; Don Van Heest, navigator; James Kennedy, bombardier. Kneeling: Gunners Chas Higgs, Howard Rackett, Richard Dunham, Don Slumpff, James Hoestman, James Pocsatko.
W. Longanecker/113 Association

set as 'unlimited', The tour of combat for the NLS, however, was set at 250hr of combat time. Flying awards were made as follows:

Air Medal	40hr of combat
1st Oak Leaf Cluster	80hr of combat
2nd Oak Leaf Cluster	120hr of combat
3rd Oak Leaf Cluster	160hr of combat
4th Oak Leaf Cluster	200hr of combat
5th Oak Leaf Cluster	240hr of combat

Distinguished Flying Cross

This was not an automatic award as some members of the squadron thought, but given only for acts of extraordinary achievement whilst on air operations.

PX Ration Cards

Post Exchange ration cards were available for periods of eight weeks at a time. They were issued by name and number to each individual on the squadron. To have more than one PX card was a court martial offence!

Fuel

Wood, coal and coke for the 'pot-bellied' stove that was in each man's quarters was available on each site — in theory. But, it was treated as gold for it was hard to obtain. In fact many night 'ground operations' were carried out by members of the squadron when they set out under cover of darkness to raid the coal/coke store. Don Childress' crew even used Very Pistol flares in their fire one cold evening! Col Aber was not amused, however, when he saw the base illuminated as the flares came out of the crew's chimney!

Bicycles

Government-issue bicycles were a boon. They were not available to combat crews, so were often bought from civilians. When finished with, they were traded in for other goods or sold to the highest bidder. All bicycles had to be fitted with a white front light and red rear light, and could not be ridden on grass or the walkways. Many however ended their days 'MIA', after failing to complete the return leg of the mission home from the pub and along the nearby canal towpath.

Orderlies

These were available to officers for 10/- or £1.00 per week, depending on the quarters occupied. The fee had to be paid promptly to Lt Hlava the Supply Officer, each month.

Gas Masks

These had to be worn, adjusted to the face, from 10.00 to 18.30hrs on the last Wednesday of each month.

Equipment

Each aircraft was fitted with the following communications equipment:

● 10 Headsets
● 10 Throat Microphones

- One B-458 Transmitter for contacting the control tower on 5770Kcs.
- Four crystals for the VHF SCR-522 set
- Flash-lights
- 10 Oxygen Mask Microphones
- One Liaison set for contacting MF/DF Stations and Operational Control. Also to monitor 4795Kcs in the event of a recall message being sent, weather changes or airfield diversions. One Command set for contacting all control towers in the UK.
- One VHF set for navigational aid, air-sea rescue and communication with Cheddington
- One Inter-phone for contact with all crew members. As well as inter-crew communication, its use was essential when oxygen was being used. Each crew position was contacted regularly by the co-pilot to ensure that there were no problems being caused by frozen masks. The crew member concerned would not be aware of this problem until he passed out. This was the case with Sgt Ed Szymczak, who suffered oxygen loss whilst on a mission on 11 March 1945; as a result he died
- One Gee set as a navigation aid
- One Boozer set. This was a device consisting of three coloured lights that were monitored whilst on missions over both enemy and Allied continental territory, where night-fighters could lurk; and also where the Wurtzberg chain of flak and ground control stations were located, a dim red light indicated the enemy was tracking them. A bright red=flak; a yellow light=enemy fighters in the area
- One IFF set to show if an aircraft was 'Friend or Foe'. As this device could be monitored itself by the enemy, its use was restricted to emergency situations only

- One Radio Compass for homing in on low-frequency beacons, but this was not used on missions. Two sets used, however, were Loran and the SCS-51. Loran was a long-range Gee set, capable of some 1,000 miles range at night, but slightly inferior to the usual Gee set. The SCS-51 was a blind-landing system that aided night landings in unfavourable weather conditions. Its disadvantage was that, unlike Cheddington, very few airfields were equipped with the ground station for its use
- Ten heated flying suits. Originally all heated suits were pooled and a crew member could be issued with as many as seven suits for as many missions. As the months went by the supply department obtained enough to make a personal issue of one set to each man. The only item pooled then was the A-3 chest-pack parachute. This pooling was not due to shortage, but to enable 10-day inspections and 30-day repacks to be accomplished.

For each mission, a Communications Section Officer or NCO would brief all crews and ensure each radio operator was issued with:

- The HF/DF station to contact and the call-sign
- All Control Tower coded call-signs — Cheddington being 'Hillside'
- Resin Light colours for that time period
- The arbitrary QFF for decoding weather reports
- The Operational W/T call-sign for the mission, and the collective call-sign of those aircraft involved
- The R/T call-sign for all aircraft
- The beacons being used
- The Gee coding and other data required to use the Gee system
- All Occults and Pundits
- All recognition signals for the period of the flight
- Flak Helmets: each aircraft in the 8th AF was authorised three flak helmets, but NLS aircraft were issued with six!
- Pistols: all crews should have been issued pistols for their own use before arriving at Cheddington. If anyone had not, they were issued one on arrival.

As well as the rules for the use of equipment, there were also rules for the Equipment Section:

- Officers and EM were not allowed beyond the service counter in the Equipment Room, without permission from any authorised personnel of the department
- Each individual was given a number which was his, bin and hanger number. Equipment was called for by that number
- Heated suits or parachute packs could not be left in the bins they had to be put in their respective places in the drying room
- Heated gloves and shoe-inserts had to be attached to the heated suit when left to dry after each mission
- Oxygen masks had to be washed on completion of a mission and also left to dry on hooks over each respective bin
- Faulty or lost equipment has to be replaced at a time other than that of take-off time

Supply Section

Like the Equipment Section, the Supply Section also functioned with a set of rules. Laundry for enlisted men had to be turned in to the Supply Room every Tuesday and was returned 10 days later. Each man was allowed nine pieces a week with a pair of socks being counted as one item, and three handkerchiefs the same! Mattress covers and fatigues could be turned in on the same day and were not deducted from the allowance. Only one pair of fatigues, however, could be turned in each week, no matter how much oil or grime they had accumulated from the constant work on the Fortress or Liberators. Fatigues and dry cleaning had to be marked with the letters 'TT', together with the last four numbers from the individual's service number. TT was also the identification mark for shoe repair tickets, as the 406th Squadron designation was never allowed to be marked on any item of clothing or equipment, in case the user came into contact with the enemy. Dry cleaning had to be turned in each Sunday and was also returned after 10 days. Regulations forbade the use of 100 octane gas (aircraft fuel) as a cleaning agent for uniforms, and violators were punished severely if caught.

Training

It was agreed by most on the airfield that the proverbial 'band of providence' a mere strong effort of will, or the lucky rabbit's foot

in the back pocket, were not enough to assure the successful completion of a tour of combat. Training, even though it brought restless sighs of boredom, was the only way to be prepared for nightfighters, flak and searchlights. It also kept at bay the authors of that War Department telegram 'We regret to inform you that your son . . .'. Training therefore in the NLS had to be completed in the following three subjects before combat flights could be undertaken:

- At least 7½hr instruction in night vision, with gunners and radio operators in their respective positions
- A minimum of 2hr of lectures on security and prisoner-of war procedure
- 1hr of hygiene instruction

Night Vision

As most, if not all the NLS combat flying was completed at night, the squadron put a heavy emphasis on night vision training. A school was opened to ensure that the crews would be just as prepared as the enemy for night flying vision; to see them, if not before, at least in time to get in the first shot. The school's purpose was to make the combat students 'blind as bats'. Nature has seen to it that the eyes best suited to night work are those in nocturnal creatures, for example the bat and the owl. These creatures are born with 'night eyes' which have evolved differently to the 'day eyes' of most other creatures. All humans have 'bat elements' in the outer portions of their eyes that are little used in daytime, and by training, the school taught how to use these parts to see better at night.

It was discovered that the ability to see on a flight in daylight was accomplished because human eyes are naturally adapted for day vision which is binocular and central, or 'foveal'. To see an object in daylight we use the optical centres of the eyes, giving colour and detail. Below moonlight, this central portion is blind and off-centre, and so peripheral vision must be employed, resulting in perception of motion, contrast and size, but not detail or colour.

Therefore seeing at night is a much different and more difficult matter than in daylight, and necessitates special training to develop and use the peripheral or parafoveal 'night portions' of the retina which are normally neglected by civilised man.

After crews had been trained in daylight for their specific jobs, they were quickly adapted for night work by the school. This was with the exception of a small handful who turned out to be 'night-blind', and who were weeded out by the standard SAM, Heehct-Sabler, RAF Hexagon or Heyford night tests. Training was carried out in a completely blacked-out building, which has shutter-controlled lighting to simulate any degree or angle of night illumination, such as high, low, right or left moonlight, half moonlight or starlight. When used with relief maps this controlled, but variable, illumination made the teaching of night aerial observation of terrain possible. The same lighting system was used in an apparatus for several off-centre eye exercises. Also in the same building were a night-simulating epidiascope (an instrument use to teach estimation of range and recognition of aircraft and ground targets) and a cine projector.

Lectures were given to between six and 12 crew members at a time and consisted of basic anatomy, physiology, and physics of night sight. They were told what dark adaptation was and how to preserve it while in searchlight cones. They were taught the tactical value of low light contrast and scanning, what the basic principles of ground and aerial night observation were, and what part constitutional factors, such as oxygen, played in eyesight. How to seek and how to avoid a foe over water, land, above or below cloud, in clear or hazy conditions of moonlight, and at what range enemy aircraft could be spotted. Constant use was also made of a RAF night gunnery (Lamplough) trainer. It presented an erratically moving (in a horizontal plane) night aerial target which, due to the low illumination, students had to follow using their parafoveal vision. The American Done trainer was preferred, but was unobtainable.

The final step in the training was when the students were blindfolded and had to familiarise themselves with every surrounding of their particular stations in the aircraft. Then, after being given the 10 Commandments of Night Sight, they had to memorise and follow them until they were prepared, and forewarned, for what to expect in combat.

Above:
Don Childress, his ground and aircrew with *Channel Fever Baby*. Don was elected to confront Maj Aber about the feelings of the squadron on promotion — or the lack of it. Many felt Don's departure from the ETO on completion of his tour was held up by this confrontation with Aber.
D. Childress/113 Association

Gunnery Training

Each day, whilst the crews were on combat training at Cheddington, they were expected to climb out of their comfortable beds and attend lectures on aircraft recognition, radio, tactics, ammunition loadings and maintenance. They also kept their hand in on the Skeet range which involved a moving target fired upon by .5in guns mounted in a turret. Guns were cleaned each day, and every 24hr they were inspected; ammunition was inspected once a week. There was also great detail given to where to look for the enemy by each gunner as follows:

● **Tail Turret:** watch from eight to four o'clock, concentrating on high areas
● **Left Waist Turret:** cover all areas as high and as low as possible, between eight and three-thirty
● **Right Waist Turret:** also as high and as low as possible, plus between four and two-thirty
● **Chin Turret:** area between ten-thirty and two-thirty on the aircraft's bow, concentrating and varying the search between high and low areas
● **Top Turret:** 360°cover with particular attention being height, and above the tail between three o'clock and nine o'clock
● **Ball Turret:** keep turret depressed below horizontal position

so that while searching low, the ball turret gunner can see no part of the underside of his aircraft. The search was made from four o'clock to eight o'clock, varying the angle of depression occasionally to 80°. A final reminder was given to all gunners not to search the other crew members' positions, as a few minutes' loss of cover could cause the enemy to attack without being seen — and could result in death!

Nightfighter Attacks

In case of attack by nightfighters whilst on leaflet raids, gunners were trained to be ready to open fire instantly and at the same time call over the intercom what evasive action the pilot should take. For dead astern attacks between five-thirty and six-thirty it would be either a right or left-hand corkscrew, according to the angle of attack. For attacks between six-thirty and nine o'clock the gunner would fire then call 'dive left!', remembering always to turn into the attack in order to give the attacking pilot a maximum deflection shot.

Lights Over Enemy Territory

Should a light be seen by a gunner who could not be certain if it was a star, a motionless light on the ground or a moving light in the sky, he was taught to position the light in his ring sight and then check for any apparent motion. He was told not to alarm his pilot by calling out numerous reports that could be unconfirmed, unless he was sure. If a nightfighter was spotted, the gunner, if possible, would check to see if it was showing any lights. The reason for this was that most twin-engined German fighters used either red, green or white lights to signal another fighter to join in the attack. If the fighter was at — say — nine o'clock and showing a red, the gunner would check at three o'clock for the other fighter.

Advice was also given on two other forms of enemy lighting: flares that gave a huge orange light and that seemed to hang motionless, were dropped above Allied aircraft from higher flying German machines and would illuminate them once underneath, thus showing the enemy a good silhouette of the Allied aircraft. The second form of lighting was the searchlight. If 'coned' by an enemy searchlight the crews were told not to dive straight down whilst attempting evasive action, but to fly at full speed straight ahead in a gradual dive. If caught in one or two lights, either sideslip, dive or stall — according to what action seemed correct to the captain at that time. Crews were also reminded that a blue light was the master beam for the cone.

Enemy nightfighters did not have it all their own way against the NLS, as there were a number of claims by the Fortress and Liberator crews. There were, however, two other unfortunate 'own goal' claims made, the first being an Allied P-61 Black Widow that was shot down, and on the last day of December 1944; a Beaufighter with an American crew was also shot down by an NLS crew. A copy of the American services newspaper *Stars and Stripes* reported the shooting-down in full, which did little to keep the incident quiet!

Operation 'Infatuate'

In September 1944, with the aid of the Belgian Resistance Forces, the Armoured Division of Gen Dempsey's 2nd Army secured the city of Antwerp. The use of its port as a supply base, however, was denied to the Allied troops since the Germans had dug in well and controlled the 40-mile river approaches that led into Antwerp. The port's facilities could handle up to 40,000 tons of supplies each day. For the Allies to send cargo vessels down this route would have been suicide.

Cherbourg was the only ship-fed supply base available to the Allied forces, but it lay several hundred miles to the rear of the advancing troops, and could only send supplies to them by truck. It was therefore of the utmost importance that a major forward supply base should come into use. Field Marshal Montgomery had accepted this and stated that the Allies' need for Antwerp 'makes the capture of the Walcherens a matter of the utmost urgency'. Hitler, once he had lost Antwerp, had given his 15th Army orders to hold Walcheren Island and use it as a fortress. This order resulted in the island and its dykes, along with the Breskens Pocket — both of which straddled the river mouth — becoming an ideal holding point. More than 86,000 men, artillery pieces, and 6,000 vehicles were moved in, building up a strong resistance against any attack by Allied troops. The engagement of these enemy forces by units who had been involved in the fight for Antwerp had been delayed for two reasons. First, Montgomery had decided to gather all his available forces and attempt a Rhine crossing before winter came. Second, an order to tie up large numbers of men, or expend large amounts of ammunition in breaching the strongly defended islands, could wait, for there were other plans to be used first — Operation 'Infatuate' held the key. A daylight bombing raid by the RAF, followed by a ground attack by British Commando forces. The time had now come for its implementation.

Walcheren was saucer-shaped and rimmed by high sand dunes, with a flat lowland interior, most of which was below sea level. There were gaps in these dunes that were filled by dykes, the largest located near Westkapelle at the western end of the island. The RAF was given the task of bombing the dykes, as it was these that held back the heavy tide of the North Sea. It was expected that, as a result of breaching them, most of the interior — including the German garrison city of Middelburg — would be flooded under 3 to 6ft of sea water. The raid, due to be launched on the afternoon of 3 October by 252 Lancasters and seven Mosquitoes of RAF Bomber Command, would include a second attack to strafe the enemy coastal batteries. After a period of waiting by the Allied forces, it was hoped that by this stage the Germans would be slogging around in the cold waters of the North Sea, and would either surrender or withdraw. If not, a commando raid would follow. For the Allied commanders

Above:
Lt Dale Wilkes (back, right) and crew with Liberator *This is it Men*, photographed on 25 February 1945. *D. Wilkes/113 Association*

Left:
The route that Col Aber and Maj Weil took on Operation 'Infatuate'. *113 Association*

planning 'Infatuate', there was just one last problem — 8,000 Dutch civilians! Gen Eisenhower was very concerned for them, and so ordered that all civilians who were in the projected danger zone should receive warning, in similar fashion to the Pre-D-Day leaflet raid in June by aircraft of the NLS.

By special order of Gen Eisenhower, the NLS was tasked to fly two daylight sorties. This was to ensure the accuracy of a widespread leaflet drop that would cover the main populated areas of the island. Leaflet ZH-3 was produced, warning that the Scheldt Estuary would be subjected to a long and heavy bombardment. All civilians were also told to move away from roads or military objectives and to keep off the lowlands.

Maj Aber felt that he could not miss this raid, so after selecting two crews — Maj Harry Gaddy and Capt August Weil — he announced he would fly as pilot in the No 1 aircraft with Maj Gaddy. After briefing at 14.00hrs, both crews took-off — Maj Aber in '516' at 15.48hrs, and Capt Weil in '167' at 15.55hrs. The two aircraft climbed out from Cheddington and, after meeting their escort of eight P-51 Mustang fighters, set course on Mission No 275. For the NLS it was its second anniversary on leaflet operations, and Maj Aber, his 30th mission of his second tour of combat duty.

Aber's aircraft was first to release its T-1 leaflet bombs when, at 17.05hrs, he dropped the first on Flushing, followed by Middelburg, Kapelle, Goes and Kortene. Capt Weil covered Domburg, Biggekerke, Arnemuiden and Westkraalert. Maj Aber caught some flak that was accurate, and heavy, over Flushing and Middelburg, but when his flightpath crossed that of Weil's the enemy guns followed Weil. German fighters also joined in the attack on both Fortress aircraft, but soon backed off when they saw the Mustang escort.

On the return journey both pilots saw a fleet of ships in a bay far below, and considered that it must be the Germans preparing to evacuate. Both crews landed safe at Cheddington, Aber at 18.41hrs and Weil at 18.37hrs.

The RAF followed next with 1,262 tons of high explosives, and as a special gift for the coastal batteries, 6.7 tons of incendiaries! The seas poured in and the Dutch took to what high ground they could find, most of it in attics or on house roofs. As for the Germans, as many of their defence positions were on the high dunes, they were unharmed. To observe the effect of the raid, Spitfire PR XIXs from No 541 Squadron, RAF Benson, were dispatched on reconnaissance missions to photograph the area. Flg Off Arnold, who took off at 14.30hrs in PL850, reported back at 16.55hrs that: 'flooding had extended approx half-a-mile inland as far as Tol and Lichitore, and water was rushing through the break in the dyke at Westkappel at a considerable rate'. The PR missions flown from Benson continued each day, and on the 4th, Flt Lt Garvey in Spitfire PR XIX RM643, flying at 1,000ft, reported the flooding had extended inland for 1¼ miles. Two days later whilst flying RM637, he reported flooding had extended inland for 3 miles but was now at sea level. He also claimed what must have been a 'first' for an unarmed reconnaissance aircraft — one enemy aircraft destroyed! This claim came about when on the mission he saw two German FW190s. One gave chase and, to avoid its guns, Garvey dived his Spitfire towards a wood. When at zero level, he pulled the stick back and made a tight roll away from death! The Luftwaffe pilot, close on his tail, failed to pull up and his aircraft exploded as it hit the trees 8 miles to the east of Bruck.

A commando attack by the 'Green Berets', of the 4th Special Services Brigade, followed on 1 November, and after several days of hard, wet fighting they 'Flushed out Flushing'. By the 4th, the Island was liberated and as soon as all the mines in the harbour had been removed, the estuary was opened to Allied shipping.

The raid was a success for the Allied troops, but for the Dutch it was a disaster. Crops were ruined and due to the lack of fodder, cattle had to be killed. Most houses were uninhabitable and if not, sanitary conditions were deplorable. Great attention was given by the Press to the raid, and to try and offset the unfortunate side effects, the part played by the 'Special Leaflet Squadron' was revealed in USAAF Press releases. These were printed in the National newspapers of both England and the USA. Set against the damage caused by the water, they showed that the leaflet warnings more than made up for it, as there were very few — if any Dutch injured in the Allied attack. As for missions over Holland, Maj Aber would be back, but it would cost him his life.

Aber's Last Mission

The night missions continued and so did the losses, but they culminated on the night of 4 March 1945 in a blow that was felt by every member of the squadron. For Mission No 864, 12 aircraft were tasked to drop leaflets on targets in Germany and Holland. One of those aircraft dispatched to Holland was *Tondalayo*, with Col Aber as captain. He was tasked to drop leaflet 'XH-95', the 4 March edition of *The Flying Dutchman* newspaper over Amsterdam, Rotterdam and Utrecht. His bombardier, **Connie Morton**, recalls that flight:

'My normal pilot was Ed Leahy, but I was out of action for a time because an armour plate fell on my finger whilst working on a jammed machine gun. Ed and the rest of our crew completed their tour of combat, and returned to the States. I then flew as an

DE VLIEGENDE HOLLANDER

Right:
XH95: De Vliegende Hollander
The 110th Issue of *The Flying Dutchman*. It was this four-page issue of the Dutch newspaper that Maj Aber had dropped over Holland on the night he was killed by Allied flak.

Below:
Tests were conducted at Cheddington on a container to air-drop food. The device worked and it was used over Holland.
N. Senter/113 Association

unassigned crew member with other crews, to make up my missions, so as to complete my tour.

'My 42nd sortie was on the night of March 4th, when we went to the Netherlands. The flight went well with only some distant flak. As we headed home, I spotted flak a number of miles away in the general area of the English coast, at the point where we were to make landfall. Col Aber and I discussed it, because there had not been any enemy raids in that area for some time. I was sure it was anti-aircraft flak, and we discussed that it might be English shore or naval batteries practising. The Colonel directed me and the other crew members to keep a close watch. We were then at 20,000ft and about to cross into England at Clacton-on-Sea. At 10,000ft, just as we crossed, I spotted a German bomber coming head on towards us. I yelled "Bandit at 12 o'clock", but we didn't get a shot because the rate of closure was so fast. We almost collided and just as the German plane passed under us, we were hit by a burst from the English batteries. The hit blew in part of my bombardier's plexi-glass compartment and I was hit in the right leg, and hip, in five places. I also had small splinters in my forehead and cheeks and one small steel splinter embedded in my right eye-ball. The first blast put our right inboard engine on fire and also part of the wing area. The plane was hit again, this time in the waist area.

'The B-17 has a compartment for the bombardier in the nose, and the navigator behind him. On this flight, we had three in that compartment: Paul Stonerock our navigator, who had flown many missions; a young navigator, Billing, who was flying his first combat operation, and me.

'When I was hit, I fell slightly backwards into the navigator's area. Paul Stonerock told Billing to stay on the intercom while he assisted me. Billing said "The colonel wants a heading to Woodbridge". Woodbridge was a base equipped especially for emergencies. It had advanced communications, the runway was wider and had special lighting. Stonerock made calculations and gave the heading and the approximate time that it would take us to reach there. Just as he did this, Billing excitedly said "Colonel said bale out". With that, Billing unhooked his intercom, and started towards the escape hatch. Stonerock said to me "Are you going to be alright?" When I replied "Yes", he said "I'm gone".

'I had decided that since I was hurt and partially blinded, I would ride the plane down if we had a chance of making Woodbridge. However, as I got to the escape hatch I decided to bale out because we were burning so badly. I said a short prayer and dropped out into the night. I had on a chest-type parachute, and at first yanked the handle instead of the rip-cord. Then I realised what was happening and pulled the rip-cord. Because of my error, I had a fairly long free-fall drop before my parachute opened.

'I could not see where I was landing, and landed abruptly and with considerable force. My parachute came down over my head and body. I had landed in shallow water and in unbelievably mucky mud. I was afraid at first I had landed in some quicksand — I couldn't stand up and could hardly see, so I sat there for a minute and tried to get my bearings. Off to the right I could see the fire from the aircraft, which had crashed and exploded. At this time I had no idea how many of our crew had got out in time. I could tell from the flames that there was water between me and the plane, and I was able to determine that the water was flowing from my back, so I figured it was headed towards a bigger body of water. Off to my left I could see what appeared to be hills, so I decided to try to crawl in that direction. As I crawled my arms would go into the mud up to — or almost to — my shoulders, and I became afraid of the quicksand. I would crawl awhile then rest. The blackout was on, of course, so my thoughts were to get to land and rest.

'It never occurred to me that the anti-aircraft crews and others had seen the aircraft go down in flames. I then saw what I thought was a small light on shore, moving towards me. I yelled, but there was no answer. I began to think it was a mirage, then it seemed to come closer so I yelled again. A man's voice said, "who are you?". I replied, "I'm a Yank". The voice replied, "talk awhile". He said if he came out he would get stuck, so directed me towards him and the bank. After a time, he did come out in boots, and got me to the bank. When on the bank he, along with two other men and a woman, removed the mud from my face, and escorted me to an area where I was placed on a stretcher and put in a truck. I was then taken into Harwich. Later, the rest of the crew, who had also baled out and who had also been assisted by local villagers, came to see me. They told me Col Aber and Maurice Harper, our co-pilot, had gone in with the aircraft at 21.20hrs, and that divers had been sent down to the wreckage to recover both bodies, but had very little luck. Only a hand that belonged to Aber was found, and that was only identified by his class ring.'

A full military funeral was held at Cambridge American Cemetery within a few days, when the coffin containing the hand, escorted by members of the squadron along with many other high-ranking officers, was buried. Col Aber had been with the squadron since it entered into leaflet operations; Lt Harper had flown Spitfires in the RCAF prior to joining the US 8th AF.

Connie Morton never saw his crew again for, by the time he was ready to leave hospital, they had all returned to America. Who he did see again was Maj Harold Gaddy, Aber's replacement as the new Squadron Commander.

It had been the summer of 1944 when **Harold Gaddy** first joined the 406th, having flown across the Atlantic to Valley in North Wales, thence by train to Cheddington. The news that confronted him on arrival, though, came as a shock. He recalls:

'I was greeted by Col Aber who informed me that his squadron flew B-17s. I told him that I had been B-24 trained, had even flown one over to England, but had never been in a B-17! He told me this presented no problem and to prove it, took me out flying the next day for about 45min in a B-17. The following night I flew as a co-pilot on an operational mission in another, and from then on was the aircraft commander for all my future missions. For the Colonel this was acceptable, as I had four years' training under my belt and some 2,000hr flying time and, at 24, was a Major. I soon came to prefer the Fort to the Lib, as it was infinitely more pleasing to the eye. It was a joy to fly and could take tremendous punishment. There was also a "feel" to flying it which was simply lacking in the B-24. I can recall that we also said the B-24 was the crate the B-17 came in — but this comment provoked some severe responses!

'In March 1945, I had finished my "Tour of Combat" and was waiting around the base for the squadron to return from a mission. Aber, who by then was a Lt-Col, had gone on the mission, as he would occasionally do, when word came through that his aircraft had been shot down and had crashed on the tide-banks near the mouth of the River Stour. Throughout the rest of the night reports filtered in from surviving crew members who had baled out, but none from Aber or Lt Harper, his co-pilot. The next morning I took a B-17 and flew to a field as near as possible to the site of the crash then went to a small detachment of the Royal Navy. They took me in a launch as close as they could — probably 100yd from the site — but, due to the low tide and shallow water, I could go no further. My co-pilot, Lt Leftwich, who was with me, and I were given some rubberised coveralls. We put them on then went over the side of the launch into the water, and slogged our way to the scene. The depth varied from waist deep at first, gradually shallowing to about 8 to 10in. Upon arrival we made the sad determination that Col Aber had been killed in the crash.

'On return to Cheddington I went immediately to Col Goodrich, the Base Commander, and reported our findings. Ironically, the previous day I had received orders transferring me to Wing Headquarters, and was supposed to report there the following day. Col Goodrich asked me if I would stay and assume command of the 406th, provided he could attain the revocation of my orders. "Of course", I said, "Yes" — what Major says no to a Colonel? Besides, I was the ranking officer in the squadron, and it was clearly my duty. Thus, it was the tragic loss of Col Aber that thrust me into command of the 406th Night Leaflet Squadron. Col Aber had been a superb organiser and moreover loved his job, hence I inherited a smoothly running squadron.'

The squadron continued flying regular missions for the next few weeks until orders were received by Gaddy to transfer the squadron to Harrington in Northamptonshire. As a squadron move is not as easy as one would think, Gaddy sent Capt Weil on ahead several days in advance to aid in the preparations for the squadron's arrival, and reported that Weil did an excellent job.

Harrington

By 'peep and jeep, luck and truck' was how the move to Harrington was recorded when the men and their equipment moved by road and air on 13 March 1945. For one crew, that of Lt **Ed Canner** who flew *The Leading Lady*, it was without luck and became a tragic flight. Ed remembers:

'We loaded our personal belongings into the aircraft and I attempted to start the engines. I got three going, but the fourth one would just not start. I had been assigned two other flying officers to transport to Harrington, but as I had tried three or four times to start the engine with no luck, they left my plane and went with another crew. After about 30min, I finally got the last engine running and we were on our way. Shortly after take-off, at about 1,000ft, one of the engines failed. I cannot recall if it was the one that had been giving trouble on the ground or not. It appeared at that time that something else happened, because normally with three engines running, a B-24 could actually climb. But, even though both my co-pilot and I were on the right rudder, with the loss of that one engine we could just not maintain altitude and it was quite obvious we were going to crash. My navigator went to his station, which was below the flightdeck, and directed us towards Harrington. When I sighted the field, I called down and ordered him to come back on deck; he said he was going to shut off the equipment. I ordered him again to come back up immediately, but once more he said he was going to shut off his equipment!

Above:
Teleprint Message.
On 7 May 1945, Cheddington's teleprint room received a teleprint message. Its content was the news all were waiting for — the war in Europe was over.

Right:
Echoes of the motion picture *The Way to the Stars*: **men from the NLS throw a Christmas party for local children — December 1944.** *113 Association*

Right:
A group of Liberators taxi into the mist at Cheddington for an evening take-off.
A. Gulliver/113 Association

Below:
Harrington — General arrangement.

Far right and following pages:
Pencil sketches of scenes depicting day-to-day life at Harrington in 1945 by Richard Sizemore, a radar mechanic attached to the 801/492nd Bomb Group.

'I could not turn the plane and was therefore intending to land on the grass portion of the Base. We were coming in on a normal approach, when I saw what I believe was an out-house in the path of the plane. I remember seeing someone come out of the out-house running as fast as he could, trying to get out of our way. At the time it looked very funny.

'When it appeared that we would not make the airfield, I called for the wheels to come down. The engineer put the wheel lever down and as they came into the slipstream they slowed the plane just enough so that we landed probably two seconds sooner than I had expected. Both wheels were down, but one wheel was not locked. When we hit the ground the aircraft was flying at about 125mph and the unlocked wheel just folded up. The whole thing just rolled — I remember going end over end for what appeared to be quite a long way. The wing fell off and caught fire, but

fortunately it was about 20yd away from the cockpit. The cockpit section I was in was probably no more than about 12ft long and had five people in it.

'Dutch, my navigator, had waited too long to come out of his navigation quarters and was killed instantly when we hit the ground. When the plane stopped rolling the cockpit section was upside down. The instrument panel was still there, but nothing was in front of it. I had my seat belt on and when I released it, I fell to the ground and simply walked out of the side of the aircraft. There was no more aluminium on the side of the plane, it had all been worn away by the tumbling.

'When I got out of the aircraft I noticed that when I bent over my back hurt, but when I stood up straight, I had no pain. I ran to the aft section of the aircraft that held at least three of my men. It was very close to the fire and when I got to it, the 0.50 calibre

Repairing a 'Lib'.

The Chow Line at the Mess Hall.

machine guns on board started to explode and I took-off. Probably within two minutes of the crash, a fire engine was on site along with an ambulance. They put me on a stretcher and carried me to hospital.'

Ed was given X-rays and found to have had a compression fracture of the first and second lumbar vertebrae. After being fitted with a plaster cast, he was flown back to America and home.

When both the air and ground sections of the 406th arrived at Harrington, the squadron set up camp — and camp it was, for both the officers and enlisted men had to sleep in tents that were erected in 'Mud City'. It was so wet and damp around the site that the men had to build small moats to carry the rainwater away. One officer even grew mushrooms under his bedding!

March had been a busy as well as tragic month, with missions on 24 out of the 31 nights. Of the six non-operational nights, two were stand-downs whilst the squadrons moved from Cheddington to Harrington, and the other four scrubs were due to poor weather. The missions flown were to France, Holland, Germany, Luxembourg and Belgium.

For the next few months, the 406th — which was no longer an independent squadron, but attached to the 492nd Bomb Group — continued its leaflet task night after night, as and when required. There had also been some extra tasks for the crews, one was that of dropping carrier pigeons! Some were dead and had false messages attached to their legs, the idea being to mislead the enemy when he found the birds. The live ones — that is those who not only survived the flight but also the descent — were used for Resistance groups to send messages back to London (that is if they could ever fly again). Pilot Dale Wilkes recalled how he plucked souvenir feathers from the frightened birds — without

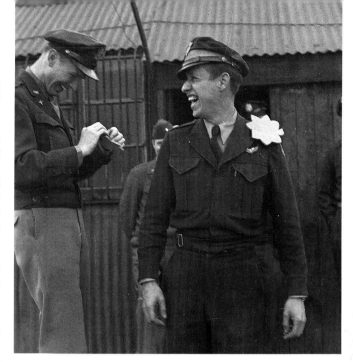

Above:
Lt-Col Harry Gaddy promotes Al Weil to the rank of Major.
B. Gunderson/113 Association

Below:
Ed Canner's crew of *The Leading Lady*. Standing, left to right: Lts 'Dutch' Cohoorn, Ed Canner, Marcina Parker-Butts and Mike Markovitch. Kneeling, left to right: Gunners Jim Mancuso, Walter Mark, Reuben Hill, Jim Keaton, Ralph Featherstone and Chas Bunnell. 'Dutch' Cohoorn was the only member killed in the crash at Harrington when the squadron moved from Cheddington.
E. Canner/113 Association

Base Radar Shack.

View from my hut, Barrack Site No 3.

telling other crew members. So did his navigator, and the bombardier and the tail gunner... The first 'Pigeon Raid' was on the night of 11 April. Aircraft flown by Lts Callaghan, Pard and Pardue, in addition to their normal bomb-load of leaflets, carried 10 'live' pigeons each. These were parachuted out over three German towns in the hope that, when retrieved, they would fly back to their homing cotes in Times Square, Piccadilly Circus, London. During the remainder of April, 340 additional pigeons in groups of 10 were all dropped over strategic and tactical targets in Germany.

In addition to leaflets and pigeons, there were a number of other 'special deliveries' by the NLS, including forged German ration cards. These were dropped to inflict severe strain on the German economy. This came about when large numbers of the public, unaware of the deception, descended on their local butcher or grocer and bought up all the available supplies with the forged cards. Another item delivered by the efficient services of the now well known 'News Boys', were 'Braddocks'. These were celluloid 3in square time-fused incendiary devices that, when dropped behind German lines, could be planted in homes or factories by civilians who were against the Nazi regime.

The original concept was Winston Churchill's, but was dropped when RAF Bomber Command, under AM Arthur 'Bomber' Harris, refused permission for RAF aircraft to carry the bombs. Those in command of PsyWar jumped at the chance however, and formulated plans for the Braddocks to be dropped with instructions for use in various languages. Also enclosed were suggestions for targets that were easily accessible by the foreign workers, and who were on the Allies' side. The use of the Braddocks had another sinister purpose. Once the enemy knew about their existence, it was possible for large fires or explosions to be blamed on the incendiary devices when they were not the actual cause. This created suspicion between German workers and their police. One of the requirements for the Braddock was that they should not be dropped within a radius of 25 miles of any POW camp. This became impossible by April 1945, and so their use was discontinued.

With an end to the hostilities, 'Tactical PsyWar Runs' came to a close, but were soon replaced by 'SHAEF Runs'. These were leaflet sorties to drop news sheets printed in English, French, Russian or Polish, to keep the many displaced people and foreign nationals up to date with current news and any important

Working at the Fuel Dump.

Red Cross Club.

Right:
Walt Longanecker Jr (second left) and his crew pose for the camera at Charleston AFB, South Carolina, in September 1944 prior to posting and assignment to the 406th Bomb Squadron at Cheddington. *W. Longanecker*

Above and right:
B-24J of the 36th Bomb Squadron, photographed from Jack Wrenn's aircraft.
M. Wrenn/113 Association

Left:
Lt Perisie's crew alongside B-24 42-94673. They were a late crew to the European theatre, but still sported early Air Force wings on their flying suits.

Below:
Lt Mould's crew in 1944 with their B-24 *Miss Stardust*. Standing, left to right: Ed Larson, Warren Paul, Harry Sandmark, Eugene Mould. Kneeling: Ken Bailey, Dave Charter, Wesley Hill, Tom Thomas, Harry Glaser . . .
113 Association

Bottom:
. . . and in August 1985.
113 Association

military instructions being released. The squadron's last leaflet mission took place on the night of 6/7 May, when 10 Liberators were dispatched to France, Holland and the Channel Islands. Once this task had been completed the war-weary crews could still not put up their feet, for there was another task to be undertaken. One that not all the men agreed with or indeed understood the reason for.

The Base Commander at Harrington, who had been a graduate of the US Military Academy at West Point, took immediate action to see that his troops did not get into mischief because of idleness. His first step was to announce that there would be a Saturday inspection of all squadrons, quarters, grounds, equipment and personnel. Harold Gaddy, who had been a flying cadet at Randolph Field and who had observed these 'West Pointers' in action, knew the matter of inspections was very important to them. So, along with his Executive Officer David Usser, whom he classed as competent and highly conscientious, he set about following the inspection requirements. By the following Saturday, everything was in first-class condition in the 406th, including the quarters, grounds and equipment. They even had their men in fresh, clean uniforms. The Base Commander was extremely pleased, which made Gaddy very proud indeed of his squadron.

The next few weeks were busy times indeed for his men, accomplishing much-needed maintenance, attending classes and lectures and generally retracing their way back to a 'spit and polish' military organisation. When the orders came for the squadron to return to America, all was in fine order. The orders, dated 28 June, directed that the squadron depart via Valley in North Wales on the best available route to Bradley Field, then on to Camp Miles Standish, Boston, which was the Port of Embarkation (P of E). This was for rest and recuperation prior to any further assignment. Thus the 20 aircrews left Harrington and flew home, with Gaddy in the lead aircraft but only this time he crossed the Atlantic from east to west and in a Fortress! The remainder of the groundcrews who could not find space on the aircraft followed later by sea.

As 'the Mouth' of PsyWar during World War 2, the Night Leaflet Squadron had used a weapon that many did not know existed, but which was so successful and efficient that its use continues to this day.

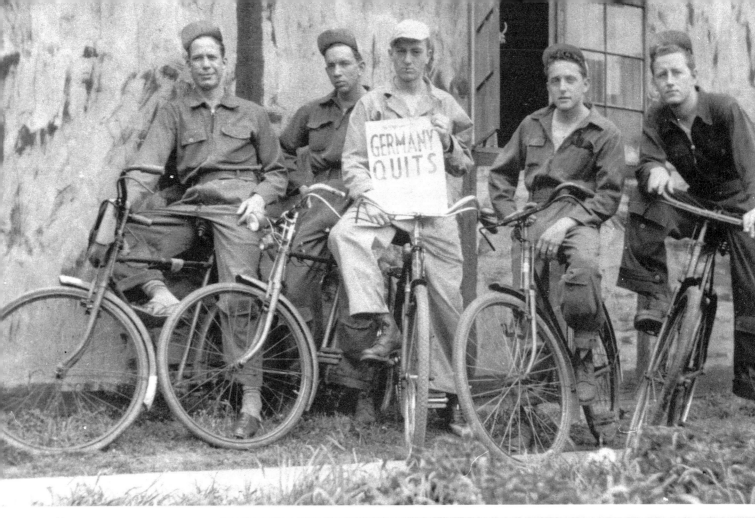

Above:
'Germany Quits' – the long and hard-fought struggle to crush Nazism is over.

Right:
Reaping the whirlwind – scenes of devastation in Germany photographed at the war's end on one of the many 'Cook's Tours' for groundcrews and non-flying personnel.

V
THE EARS

No 100 Group RAF

From the outbreak of war, RAF Bomber Command sent its aircraft far into the enemy homeland without the protection of countermeasures against any form of enemy radar, the reason being that at that time the Allies had no proof of its existence. Evidence, however, started to come to light from December 1939, when an aerial that had been removed from the scuttled German pocket battleship *Graf Spee* at Montevideo was examined by a British radar expert. A second clue came with the repeated use of the word *Freyer* in intelligence reports that were received during the middle period of 1940. *Freyer* was finally uncovered as a radar, in February 1941, when its frequency was located and identified. This allowed the plotting of *Freyer* sites by British radio operators searching the frequency bands, and by October a total of 27 sites had been located. In less than a month, another site at Bruneval had been located by aerial photography. This caused much excitement because the site contained a new type of radar. As the site was located close to the French coast it allowed for the now-famous Operation 'Biting' to take place, when 119 men were parachuted in from Whitley aircraft. This raid resulted in 17 British casualties, but also the capture of three German operators who, along with their radar receiver, amplifier, modulator, transmitter and aerial, were brought to England for interrogation and examination. The Germans, who expected a second raid to take place, increased the security of all the other sites and surrounded them with barbed wire. This move however, made the sites more conspicuous from the air, thus aiding the photographic reconnaissance Spitfires and Mosquitoes from RAF Benson and allowing more intelligence to be gathered by the Allied forces. As a result, by July 1942 a good picture had been built up of enemy radar operations.

If there was any doubt as to the German ability to jam British radar, it was removed on 11 July 1942 when the German cruisers *Scharnhorst* and *Gneisenau* sailed up the English Channel. This provocative act was accomplished in broad daylight whilst jamming the British radar systems to avoid attack. It resulted in the start of British offensive radar countermeasures (RCM), and a race to produce equipment, test it, then form squadrons to put it to use. RAF Fighter Command was the first off the blocks, with aircraft equipped with 'Moonshine' jammers. These, developed by the Telecommunications Research Establishment (TRE), pro-

duced spurious returns on the enemy's *Freyer* early warning radar system. It worked by re-transmitting the *Freyer* signal, and therefore increasing the strength of the 'spoof' echo. Bomber Command took over the lead in the race with the formation of No 100 Group on 8 November 1943, and used the previously formed No 80 Wing as a foundation. This Wing, based at Radlett in Hertfordshire and under the command of AVM Addison, had commenced testing of prototype equipment. The Group's brief was to operate airborne and ground RCM equipment to deceive or jam enemy radar systems, wireless signals, and radio navigation equipment. It was also to examine all intelligence on enemy radar systems and radio navigation equipment, to enable tactics or modifications to be made to Allied aircraft or operations.

The Group's first operational unit was No 141 Squadron, formed on 3 December 1943 at West Raynham, and equipped with Beaufighter VIf and Mosquito Mk II aircraft. By mid-January 1944, No 100 Group consisted of the following squadrons and flights:

- No 141 (SD) Squadron — Beaufighter, Mosquito
- No 169 (SD) Squadron — Mosquito
- No 192 (SD) Squadron — Wellington, Halifax, Mosquito
- No 239 (SD) Squadron — Mosquito
- No 515 (SD) Squadron — Beaufighter, Defiant
- No 1473 (SD) Flight — Anson
- No 1692 (SD) Flight — Beaufighter, Defiant.

Sculthorpe

The first 'Heavy' squadron to join the Group was No 214 at Sculthorpe, Norfolk, on 17 January 1944. This squadron had been equipped with four-engined Short Stirling aircraft, but was converting to the American B-17 Flying Fortress. To convert crews on to the Fortress, No 1699 Flight was formed. Its staff put the ex-Stirling crews through seven days of ground training, followed by 25hr flying time. This time included air firing, fighter affiliation and cross-country flights. Following a 'Bullseye' sortie, pilots went on a 'second dickey' operation as second pilot with an experienced crew, before returning to their own crew for their first operation together.

The use of the B-17 came about because of its performance and suitability, plus its availability. The decision to use the type was made at HQ RAF Bomber Command, High Wycombe, when several requirements were drawn up.

- RAF Bomber Command requested the supply of 14 B-17 aircraft from the US 8th AF, plus replacements. These aircraft were to be replaced in American service by an equal number of B-17G aircraft, off-set from future British Lend-Lease contracts.
- In terms of electronic equipment, each aircraft would carry H2S, Gee or Loran, API and AMU, a DR compass, 'Monica' IIA, MF and HF communications, HF and VHF R/T, 'Jostle IV' and four 'Airborne Grocers'. The installation of 'Jostle' and 'Airborne Grocer' would be acceptable.
- Each aircraft would carry a rear, mid-upper and ball turret gunner.

With regard to aircraft performance, the following estimates were arrived at: aircraft complete with all electronic equipment and armament having an overall weight of 60,500lb (27,442kg) — a range of 1,150 miles (1,851km) at 135mph (217km/hr) at an operational height of 30,000ft (9,144m). A range of 1,400 miles (2,253km) at 215mph (346km/hr) at an operational height of 25,000ft (7,620m). For an aircraft without H2S or vertical turret, and having an overall weight of 59,000lb (26,762kg) — a range of 1,220 miles (1,963km) at 230mph (370km/hr) at an operational height of 30,000ft (9,144m). A range of 1,500 miles (2,414km) at 212mph (341km/hr) at an operational height of 25,000ft (7,620m).

Above:
Sgts Jim Fettig, Bob Lathrop and Johnny Redd on 'station' transport.
B. Downs/113 Association

Left:
One of the first RAF Fortress aircraft to be fitted with ECM equipment by Scottish Aviation at Prestwick. The aerials flanking the twin tail guns are 'Airborne Grocer', and 'Monica' below the guns.
IWM ATP13090D

Below left:
Fortress 'BU-S' No 214 Squadron RAF shows proud its H2S radome beneath its nose. In the background is 'BU-U'. *RAF Museum PO17128*

The crew would comprise a pilot, navigator, flight engineer, wireless-operator, special operator, bombardier (to act as second navigator/air gunner), and two air gunners.

The first B-17, 41-24577, arrived on 20 January 1944, and was used for conversion training and then fitted with jamming equipment. To train the English air and groundcrews of No 214 Squadron on the American aircraft, a small detachment of men from the 8th AF was moved into Sculthorpe. On 28 March, General Order No 5 was issued from AFCC at Cheddington, directing that the detachment would become the 803rd (Provisional) Bomb Squadron (H). Under the command of Capt Paris, the squadron was then deemed to be the 8th AF RCM detachment. At first the squadron was involved purely with the training of English crews, but within a short time efforts were taken to integrate them with those of the RAF, and for the RAF to provide its initial equipment. On 10 February, six crews arrived with their B-17s from the 96th Bomb Group, 8th AF, who had all completed their 25-mission tour of combat. They had been selected from a number of other crews at Snetterton Heath who were due to return home to America. These six crews, therefore, were all new to each other and unused to each other's way of work. This formation caused morale to fall like a stone!

By 1 April, the following equipment had been fitted into the B-17s:

one aircraft — three 'Carpet' sets, one 'Mandrel' set;
two aircraft — four 'Mandrel' sets;
two aircraft — six 'Mandrel' sets;
one aircraft — one 'Blinker', one S27, one SCA587.

Above:
A 'Boozer II' indicator unit fitted on to the instrument panel of a B-24. A red light indicated the presence of enemy *Würzburg* radar transmissions and a yellow lamp, that of FuG 202/212 transmissions. *Royal Signals & Radar Establishment, Malvern (RSRE)*

Left:
A selection of 'Mandrel' antennas from the T1408 A to the T1408 F. Each antenna was cut to the required length for the frequency range being jammed, and mounted under the aircraft's wing. 'Mandrel' was essentially a standard IFF set, altered so that it could receive and transmit continuously. When an enemy signal was received, the set was switched to transmit thus jamming the incoming signal. *RSRE*

Left:
A 'Carpet II' control unit fitted in a B-25 Mitchell by the TRE for research and trials. 'Carpet' was used to spot jam *Würzburg* gun laying and GCI radars. An operator made a sweep of the frequency range and when a signal was found, its frequency was tuned into the transmitter and the signal jammed with noise. *RSRE*

Below left:
T1630 transmitters fitted into the TRE's B-25 for research and trial work. *RSRE*

Below:
A close-up view of a 'Jostle' transmitter. 'Jostle' was used for continuous frequency modulated jamming of enemy R/T. The turning heads covered from 17 to 54mc/s. *RSRE*

Above:
A RAF officer and a NCO stand beside their American bomb truck, modified to carry the 'Jostle' transmitter in a vertical position to the aircraft dispersal point. *RSRE*

Left:
When at the dispersal it was lowered into a specially dug pit. The aircraft was then brought over the pit and the jammer winched up into the bomb bay. *RSRE*

87

Right:
A 'Jostle' T1524 transmitter fitted into a B-17 bomb bay. It measured 51in high, 24.5in in diameter, weighed 600lb, and its case was maintained at a pressure of 35lb/sq in. *RSRE*

Below:
The B-17 Special Radio Operator's section showing a T11991A wavemeter, a Type 2000 visual display unit, and alongside, a 'Jostle' control panel. Fortress and Liberator aircraft were the only types that could carry 'Jostle'. *RSRE*

Oulton

On 25 April, Capt Paris became the Operations Officer and handed command of the squadron over to Maj Scott. A further change occurred on 16 May when RAF Sculthorpe was closed, and both Nos 214 and 803 Squadrons moved to RAF Oulton, some 20 miles away. At the time of this move considerable thought had been given to the use of the 803rd on operations, and so its aircraft were equipped with 'Carpet' and 'Mandrel' jammers, and its crews trained to operate them.

The squadron's first operation came on the night of 5/6 June 1944, when along with other aircraft of No 100 Group, a 'Mandrel' screen was put up by four 803rd B-17s to mask the progress of the Allied invasion fleet, heading towards the French coast. The aircraft took off at 22.00hrs and started to jam at 22.35hrs. They continued until 04.50hrs, then returned safely to Oulton. Operations continued into June with the 803rd sending 27 aircraft out on five nights to provide a screen for RAF bombers. Of the 31 sorties, 28 were effective as there was one abort on the 22nd and two on the night of the 27th. The screens were flown at 15,000ft until the night of the 27th, when tactics were changed and the height increased to 19,000ft. This height was maintained during July, when 58 sorties were flown on 14 nights. On 12 July the 803rd sent its first B-24 Liberator out on a mission. The Liberator was destined to replace the squadron's Fortresses for it was now accepted to be a more suitable aircraft for RCM operations. The changeover to an all-Liberator fleet was completed by 28 July.

36th Bomb Squadron (RCM)

August saw more changes, including a new Commanding Officer, Maj Hambaugh, who had been the squadron's Liaison Officer with No 100 Group RAF, also a new type of mission, with 'spoof' sorties being flown. The main change was on the 13th, when the 803rd merged with the 856th Bomb Squadron, changed its designation to the 36th Bomb Squadron (H) (RCM), and moved to Cheddington alongside the NLS, sharing its Operations Room. The Operations Room was not the only item that the 36th shared with another unit. Whilst its Liberators made lone patrols, adorned with the new squadron code 'R4' painted on their fuselages, other aircraft lurked in the night. Was it accidental or intentional on the part of the 8th AF that those letters were the same ones used by the Luftwaffe nightfighter unit *Nachjagdge-schwader 2* (NJG 2). This unit had been formed in September 1940, with its *Gruppen* (Squadrons) and *Stab* (Headquarters Flight) using Dornier Do17Z-10, Do215B-5, Do217J-1 and Junkers variants, including the G6b.

The remainder of August saw 'Mandrel' operations continue including four ELINT (Electrical Intelligence) gathering sorties, where radio bands and frequencies were searched to locate those in use by the enemy. The 'Mandrel' screens were in support of RAF raids to Germany (six), France (five), and one 'spoof' raid. The same format continued into September with 87 aircraft being dispatched on 'Mandrel' duties. The 'Mandrel' screen was now a 'creeping' screen on all missions, unlike the original sorties that remained stationary and did not move towards the enemy coast. Work also continued on navigation training and the staffing of a 'Special RADAR School' that had been opened at Cheddington to train radio operators from other Bomb Groups in the operation of 'Mandrel', 'Monica' and 'Jostle' jammers.

Above:
RCM cover for Operation 'Overlord' — 5/6 June 1944.

RCM cover for Operation 'Overlord' — the Allied invasion of France — consisted of five separate operations:

> 1. 'Taxable'
> 2. 'Glimmer'
> 3. 'ABC'
> 4. 'Titanic'
> 5. 'Mandrel'

'TAXABLE'
A combined naval and air diversion against Cap d'Antifer with 16 aircraft from No 617 Squadron RAF.

'GLIMMER'
As with 'Taxable', 'Glimmer' was also a joint naval/air operation but against Boulogne. No 218 Squadron RAF provided six aircraft.

'ABC'
Operations consisted of 24 aircraft from No 101 Squadron RAF along with five aircraft from No 214 Squadron providing VHF jamming support for Operation 'Taxable' and 'Glimmer'.

'TITANIC'
'Titanic' consisted of 34 aircraft from Nos 90, 138, 149 and 161 Squadrons RAF, which provided three feint airborne attacks towards Caen.

'MANDREL'
The 'Mandrel' screen was provided by 16 aircraft from No 199 Squadron RAF, and four aircraft from the 803rd Bomb Squadron USAF, consisting of two screens with 12 centres.

October saw the first 'Mandrel' screen in support of the 8th AF when, on the 10th, seven aircraft were tasked to provide a daylight screen to mask B-17 and B-24s returning from a leaflet raid. This mission set the pattern for all future sorties. The screens continued into November, providing protection for departing RAF and returning 8th AF bombers, but from the 25th, cover was extended for the 8th AF and retracted for the RAF. This was due to the gradual phasing out of involvement with No 100 Group operations. From 25 November, the 8th AF screen was also flown in daylight and used to mask radio chatter coming from the B-17 and B-24 bombers assembling prior to setting out on their bomb raids. Sorties were then flown each day until the 30th. Up to 25 November, 78 aircraft were dispatched to support RAF operations and following that date, one 'Mandrel' patrol each night. The Group Intelligence Officer summarised the missions in a short poem that said it all:

Above right:
Capt Stutzman, Lt-Col Scott and Capt Robinson of the 36th Bomb Squadron. *R. Stutzman/113 Association*

Right:
Maj Robert F. Hambaugh from Birmingham, Al, who took over the command of the 36th Bomb Squadron from Col Scott, pictured in the pilot's seat of an Airspeed Oxford. *F. Wilkins/113 Association*

Below:
Form 5 — Individual Flight Log.
Each month Form 5 was completed by the squadron's Operations Officer. Vane Glendening recorded his 52 missions with the 36th Bomb Squadron (RCM). His total operational hours of 301 worked out at 5.7hr per mission.

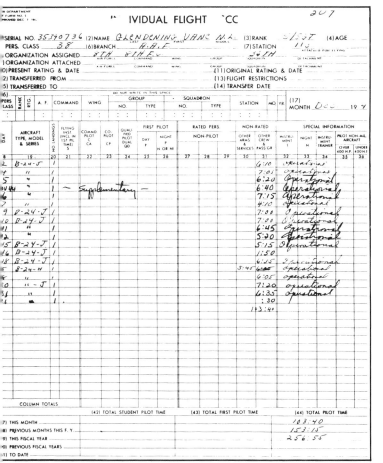

THE NIGHT OF 23/24TH NOVEMBER 1944

Bomber Command had laid on a raid,
To be carried out with 100 Group's aid.
But Bomber considered the weather was poor,
So Group took a hand at alerting the Ruhr.
They put up a suitably placed Mandrel Screen,
Through which, so they hoped, not a thing could be seen.
They sang to the Hun a Serrate serenade,
Round the beacons they danced a Perfectos Parade.
They intruded up high, they intruded down low,
(Just to be beastly they'd put on this show).
The Window force windowed 100 per cent,
And came through the screen with offensive intent.
The Hun plotted hundreds of Heavies around,
But hadn't a hope of control from the ground.
He put up some fighters and led them astray,
In a huge mass of blips that faded away.
Our immediate analysis shows in the main,
That the poor bloody Hun had been fooled once again.

In November, the first 36th Squadron crew was killed when, on the night of the 9/10th, B-24 42-51226 coded R4-L, crashed. The aircraft, flown by Lt Joseph Hornsby, was returning from a mission when fire broke out in one of the four engines. Joe gave the bale-out order but for some unknown reason three crew members failed to jump. Lt Fred Grey the navigator, Sgts Ray Mears and Frank Bartho, who were both gunners, died in the abandoned aircraft when it crashed in flames near Boucly in

Northern France. A second crash occurred at 23.48hrs on the night of the 15th, whilst B-24 42-51219 coded R4-I, was taking-off for a 'Mandrel' screen mission. Norman Landberg, the captain, made a normal take-off from Cheddington's runway 08 and climbed out following the 2,000ft lane of red warning lamps which extended from either side of the runway. The aircraft cleared the railway line, but came down again about 3,000ft east of the tracks and just left of the runway centreline. The tail gunner, **George Eberwine**, recalled the crash:

'One minute we were up — the next we were down. I had my back to the bulkhead and that saved me as the Lib just folded up. After we came to a halt I just ran to get clear of what I thought would be an explosion. I then realised there were only two of us so went back to do what I could for the others whilst my buddy went for help.'

Lying dead in the shattered wreckage were the navigator, Walter Lamson, and one of the gunners, Leo Smith. The cause of the crash, following an investigation, was put down to instrument failure and pilot error.

December brought more deaths for the squadron. On the 19th, whilst returning from a mission, B-24 42-51232 coded R4-J was diverted to RAF Manston in Kent as Cheddington was 'closed in' due to fog. The crew remained there until the 22nd, when they set off for home at Cheddington. Again due to the weather, Cheddington was closed, so Bill Lehner, the B-24's navigator, gave a course for RAF Valley to his captain, Harold Boehm. The Lib with its crew of 10 set off for the Welsh airfield, but the extra flying time proved to exceed the aircraft's fuel reserves, and the crew were forced to bale out three miles southwest of Valley. Only Harold Boehm and his co-pilot Don Birch survived. The other eight crew members, whose bodies were never recovered from the Irish Sea, were reported as 'Missing In Action', presumed drowned. As for missions in December, support for the 8th AF raids continued with screens provided to mask the radio chatter

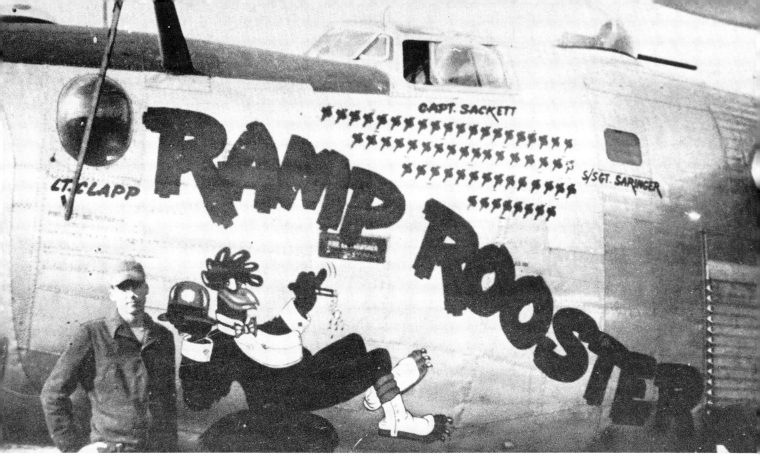

Above:
Irl Fife, the crew chief of *Ramp Rooster*, pictured at Cheddington. The lightning strike marks beneath the cockpit indicate jamming missions. *I. Fife/113 Association*

Right:
***Ramp Rooster* before her nose art was completed.** *113 Association*

Below right:
B-24J 42-51230 *LiL Pudge* and her unknown co-pilot of the time. *N. Senter/113 Association*

on 23 days, and a further nine screens provided to mask the RAF's operations.

The squadron recorded a 'first' on the 28th, when a 'Jackal' mission was flown. Liberators R4-E *Li'l Pudge*, R4-H *The Beast of Bourbon*, and R4-K *Lady in the Dark*, set course for the enemy front-line in Belgium. When the three aircraft were in position, they orbited the area for 4hr, jamming enemy army vehicle and tank radios that were participating in the 'Battle of the Bulge'. To test how effective the jamming was, Liberator R4-N *This is it Men*, was used with an S27 search receiver which monitored the enemy frequencies. As jamming also affected Allied aircraft bombing equipment, it was stopped when Allied aircraft approached.

The year 1944 came to a very successful end for the 803rd/36th staff, who had achieved a lot in a very short time. Mission tactics had been perfected and equipment tested, approved, and installed. Commendations had been received from both 8th AF and RAF for the effectiveness of the squadron's jamming. Their aircraft were the most powerful jamming machines in Europe. But the war was not yet won and there was still a lot of work to do, both in training and equipment installations. The missions could be broken down into three types:

Right:
The Beast of Bourbon taxies past the station Control Tower. **The Beast** was lost in a take-off accident on 19 February 1945.
N. Senter/113 Association

Below right:
Rum Dum was the personal mount of Sam 'VAT '69' Ziff.
N. Senter/113 Association

Below:
Mandrel Jamming Patterns: *Racecourse* (right). A racecourse screen comprised two aircraft which flew a 10min diagonal circuit, consisting of two long and two short legs. These legs, flown up and down Gee lines, required accurate timing by the pilot and navigator in order to maintain the position of the screen.
Shifting Racecourse (left). Starting on 17 July 1944, the screen became a 'creeping mandrel', its centre slowly moving towards the enemy coast. This was achieved by making the downwind leg longer that the following upwind leg.

Mandrel:

A screen provided to mask the radio traffic caused whilst Bomb Groups were assembling, thus preventing enemy ears from having advanced indication of the numbers of Allied bombers involved.

Spoof

Three aircraft would try to deceive the enemy into thinking that a second bomber formation was assembling, by operators reading typical Bomb Group formation messages from a script.

Mandrel R/T

Jamming aircraft would travel with the Bomb Group formations towards the target to screen R/T messages.

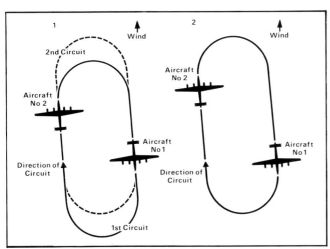

As for the jamming equipment installed in the aircraft, the situation was much more complicated and must have been very confusing for the ground crews and staff from the 476 Sub-Depot, who had been moved into Cheddington on Detached Service to fit, remove and then re-fit the equipment. The following aircraft had jamming equipment installed by the end of 1944:

Jackal	Carpet I	Jostle	Dina	Mandrel	ELINT
50665	250665	251311	250665	250385	250622
50476	250476	251315	251230	250665	250671
51230	251230		251685	250750	
51685	151685		295221	250844	
95221	401609		250385	251546	
01609	251331		251239	295221	
	251315		251308		
	251315		251576		
			250671		

In addition to the fitting of jammers, a number of other modifications were made to the aircraft. These included the installation of a floor in the right rear bomb-bay to carry the extra equipment; the fitting of overhead lighting, oxygen and flight-suit heating points for the Special Radio Operators; the fitting of the required number of aerials either under the wings or on the tail section. The ball turret was removed to be replaced by 'Jostle' jammers. The 'Jostle' itself was transported by a converted bomb-truck, then lowered into a pit that had been dug in one of the aircraft disposals. The aircraft would then be manoeuvred into position over the pit and the jammer raised into the Liberator's ball turret position.

The cold Christmas of 1944 gave way to January 1945, but there was no let-up in the missions. Out of a total of 24 missions, two 'Mandrel' screens were provided for the RAF, with the rest being the now regular VHF screening for the 8th AF. **Odis Waggoner**, a gunner in the 36th, recorded the month and his missions in his diary:

1st: We started off the New Year by flying another morning mission in 188 — Uneventful; 6hr 45min.

2nd: We had a practice mission this afternoon, testing a new antenna.

3rd: Nothing to do today. Went to the aero club with Sid and Way tonight.

4th: Nothing to do today. Went to the show on the Base tonight.

5th: Flew another mission this morning. Got back after our two-day pass had started. Went into London with Way tonight: 6hr 30min.

6th: Way and I ran around together today. Then Way, Catt, and I saw *30 Seconds over Tokio* this afternoon.

7th Returned to our Base this afternoon. Caught the 11.35 train from Euston. Walked from the crossroads outside Tring to base.

8th Flew another mission this morning in 188. Had to abort after we had been in position about an hour. Got credit for the time: 3hr 30min.

9th Flew another morning mission in 'L'. Were recalled early and I was glad −46°C at 21,000′. Had two teeth filled: 3hr 30min.

10th Nothing to do today. Lt Young's crew finished up.

11th Nothing to do today.

12th We were woken for a mission this morning but they scrubbed it before we got dressed for chow. Nothing else today.

13th Nothing to do today. Put pictures in my new album tonight.

14th Nothing to do today. Woke up late to go to church.

15th Flew another mission this morning in 'I'. Kept smelling gasoline all through flight otherwise uneventful: 6hr 15min.

16th Nothing to do today.

17th Flew another mission this morning in 'P'. Uneventful: 5hr.

Top:
Two of the 36th Bomb Squadron's B-24s taxi back after a mission.
N. Senter/113 Association

Left:
Mission plan for 2 January 1945:
1. Four aircraft Mandrel screen.
2. Three aircraft Jackal screen.

18th Nothing to do today.

19th Slow timed '188' this morning. Had a tooth filled this afternoon.

20th Flew another mission this morning in '188'. −48°C at 22,000'. Uneventful. I went into London on my class 'B' pass tonight to see *Castle Arford*: 5hr 30min.

21st Went to church this morning. Nothing to do today.

22nd Nothing to do today.

23rd Nothing to do today. Went to the show on the Base tonight, saw *Summer Storm*.

24th Flew another mission in 'F'. We were diverted to Woodbridge and then went by truck to Martlesham Heath to sleep: 5hr 15min.

25th Mission was scrubbed.

26th Flew another mission this morning in 'F'. We were diverted to Linton. No 1 engine lost oil pressure on the final approach. Need new engine: 5hr 45min.

27th We started on a mission in 'M' this morning but they scrubbed it after we got to the end of the runway. I slid off the wing whilst I was checking the gas. I broke a bone in my left hand. They took me to York and put a cast on it. I removed the cast around midnight — severe pain.

28th The pain eased this morning. Then I went back to Cheddington this evening by plane. Stayed in the hospital overnight: 1hr 45min.

That was the end of combat for Odis. He was given credit for the mission, making a total of 50 missions. His operational flying time was some 296hr 15min, and total flying time 554hr 15min.

Jamming

January may well have seen the end of operations for Odis, but for **Lee Hendrickson** it was only the start. Lee remembers:

'After sixty-eight days' training which included one hundred and one hours' transition training as co-pilot on B-24J aircraft, my crew and I departed November 1st 1944 for processing and a two-week overseas ocean voyage to Liverpool, England. Of the fifty-two crews on our shipment, half went without bombardiers, ours amongst them.

'Upon arrival in Liverpool, we were assigned and transported to the HQ 70th Replacement Depot at Army Air Force Station 594,

Below and below right:
When You Are Overseas.
A leaflet given to all American airmen prior to service in England with the 8th AF. It gave information on writing home, military mail and civil V-mail, cables, careless talk and capture!

War Department Pamphlet No. 21–1   29 July 1943

WHEN YOU ARE OVERSEAS
THESE FACTS ARE VITAL

Writing home

THINK! Where does the enemy get his information—information that can put you, and has put your comrades, adrift on an open sea; information that has lost battles and can lose more, unless you personally, vigilantly, perform your duty in SAFEGUARDING MILITARY INFORMATION?

CENSORSHIP RULES ARE SIMPLE, SENSIBLE.—They are merely concise statements drawn from actual experience briefly outlining the types of material which have proved to be disastrous when available to the enemy. A soldier should not hesitate to impose his own additional rules when he is considering writing of a subject not covered by present regulations. He also should guard against repeating rumors or misstatements. It is sometimes stated that censorship delays mail for long periods of time. Actually, mail is required to be completely through censorship within 48 hours.

There are ten prohibited subjects

1. Don't write military information of Army units—their location, strength, matériel, or equipment.
2. Don't write of military installations.
3. Don't write of transportation facilities.
4. Don't write of convoys, their routes, ports (including ports of embarkation and disembarkation), time en route, naval protection, or war incidents occurring en route.
5. Don't disclose movements of ships, naval or merchant, troops, or aircraft.
6. Don't mention plans and forecasts or orders for future operations, whether known or just your guess.
7. Don't write about the effects of enemy operations.
8. Don't tell of any casualty until released by proper authority (The Adjutant General) and then only by using the full name of the casualty.
9. Don't attempt to formulate or use a code system, cipher, or shorthand, or any other means to conceal the true meaning of your letter. Violations of this regulation will result in severe punishment.
10. Don't give your location in any way except as authorized by proper authority. Be sure nothing you write about discloses a more specific location than the one authorized.

INCLOSURES IN LETTERS.—Do not inclose anything in a letter that would violate any of the foregoing rules.

PHOTOGRAPHS, FILMS.—Special rules apply to the transmission of photographs and films. Do not send them until you have ascertained what regulations are in effect in your area.

540677°—43

2

POST CARDS.—The use of post cards may or may not be authorized. Find out first, and then be sure that the picture or printed part of the card does not violate censorship regulations.

Letter addresses

ADDRESS.—Always leave room for a forwarding address to be written in.
On mail to civilians.—Use normal address and form.
On mail to military personnel.—Give name, grade (rank), Army serial number (if known), unit and organization, and location if in United States. If addressee is also overseas use his APO number c/o Postmaster ——. If in the same general locality as the sender see Army Postal Service for authorized address.
On mail to prisoners of war held by enemy.—Obtain full information from local Army Postal Service.

RETURN ADDRESS.—Every letter or post card must have a return address. Place it in the upper left-hand corner, leaving a margin of ½ inch for resealing in case of censorship beyond the unit censor. The ½-inch margin rule applies equally to mail from officers and from enlisted men. Both are subject to examination by base censorship detachments.

Free

Sgt. John Smith, 6749318,
Co. C, 299 Inf., A. P. O. 1005,
c/o Postmaster, New York City, N. Y.

Mrs. John Smith,
123 First Avenue,
New York City, N. Y.

The return address must include (1) full name, including grade (rank), (2) Army serial number, (3) unit (company, battery, etc.), (4) organization (regiment, etc.), (5) APO number, (6) c/o Postmaster (city assigned).

Return addresses on mail written to prisoners of war are subject to specific regulations. Obtain information locally.

No geographical location of sender may be shown on an envelope or other outside cover.

Official military mail

Special regulations are provided for official military mail. They are not covered herein.

Mailing your letter

Reread your letter to be sure you have complied with all regulations. This will protect you and assure the most expeditious delivery of your letter. Five minutes now will save later delay and prevent possible suppression of the letter. It will protect you from punishment for unintentional violations.

ENLISTED MEN.—Place your letter unsealed in your organization mail box, never in any civil post office box. *You are required to use the Army Postal Service, and the Army Postal Service only.*

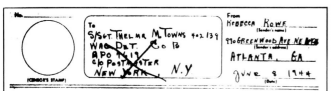

[handwritten V-Mail letter]

Dear Thelma

I am taking a chance on this — hope you get it

D Day here was very solemn. Most everyone went to church during the day or evening mass & I were asleep when the first news came at 2:30

Inez Jones is in town for a few days. She, Frances and Lois Bruce had dinner with me D Day evening. Inez looks well. She and Lois inquired about you and said to give you their love. Betty McGuire has been home and Lois says she plans to be married in the fall after graduation.

Heard Miss Emily Woodward's broadcast from England last night. It was most interesting. & hope you got to hear it.

May go out in country Saturday to pick black berries. Wish you were here to go with me.

If you need anything please let me know. ___ now to ship fried chicken

with love "Ramona"

Stone, Stafford. There we were briefed on customs and courtesies of the British people, language and behavioural differences and the avoidance of such words as 'bloody' in mixed company. We were relieved from assignment to that station on November 30th, and ordered to proceed on December 1st to Cheddington. On arrival we were assigned to a hut, furnished to our satisfaction with steel beds. These had straw-filled, three-piece "biscuit" mattresses and a pot-bellied stove for which we were rationed three and a half pounds of coke per man per day. We heated the hut from 16.30hrs to 22.00hrs each day, and felt privileged to have had the only hut on our site with adjoining toilet!

'Happy at last, after six months of continuous moves, we settled down to training. This consisted of ten flights during the month to familiarise our crew with England, foggy weather landings, navigation using Gee systems and searchlight locating of bases, and, at long last, actual practice in the use of the radio and radar-jamming equipment. After some sixteen hours of English flying weather we flew our first mission on January 6th 1945.

3

OFFICERS.—Seal the envelope, sign your name without comment in the lower left-hand corner to indicate your compliance with censorship regulations (your letter is subject to further censorship examination by base censorship detachments), and deposit in the organization mail box. *Use only the Army Postal Service.*

V-mail

This is an expeditious mail program which provides for quick mail service to and from soldiers overseas. A special form is used which permits the letter to be photographed on microfilm, the small film transported, and then reproduced and delivered. Use of V-MAIL is urged because it greatly furthers the war effort by saving shipping and airplane space. Censorship rules apply to V-mail with such adjustments as are necessary due to the form used and special processing features.

Blue envelopes

Enlisted men who wish to write of private or family matters and who feel that censorship of a specific letter by their unit censor would cause embarrassment may be authorized to use a blue envelope which will allow censorship action to be taken by the base censor rather than the unit censor. Blue envelopes should be obtained from your organization and must be addressed to the final intended recipient. Only one letter may be placed in each envelope and the envelope should be sealed prior to mailing. Censorship regulations apply to blue envelopes as well as to all other communications.

Warning

Written communications may be sent only through the facilities of the Army Postal Service. Any attempt to avoid this restriction by mailing letters in civil postal systems or by having travelers transport communications will result in severe disciplinary action against both the sender and the intermediary.

Cables; radiograms

Every cable message goes through the hands of at least 12 people. Radiogram messages are available to all who wish to "tune in," including the enemy!

Constant effort is being made to provide you with approved, rapid, cheap electrical communication.

Under no circumstances can cables be sent over commercial or foreign outlets until their use is authorized by proper military authority. "Safe Arrival" messages, identifiable as such, are prohibited at any time. There are two types of electrical messages generally available: Senders' Composition Messages (SCM's), which are like the cablegrams and radiograms you know at home, and Expeditionary Force Messages (EFM's) which are fixed text messages sent at a very low rate, much like Christmas and birthday telegraph messages in use in the United States, but with set messages composed to meet your normal requirement.

As soon as safety allows you will be assigned an APO *cable* address. Until it is assigned only serious, emergency messages may be sent, and then only if first approved in writing by the theater or area commander or his authorized representative. The Red Cross can handle certain extremely urgent personal matters by cable.

Ask your unit censor how to send messages, either SCM's or EFM's. Under no circumstances may you mention your unit or organization, or any military establishment; nor may you mention in the text any APO number other than your own.

4

Cable addresses

Outbound.—First give *your* cable address; next, the full name, street address, city, and State of the person for whom the message is intended; then the message, and finally sign your full name. Example:

AMTRAG (typical APO cable address)
Mrs. John Smith, 1616 Main St.,
Zenith, Ohio.
XXXXXX Message XXXXXX
XXXXXXXXXXXXXXXXXX
John T. Smith.

Note that addresses and signatures do not include Army serial numbers, unit or organization designation, or APO numbers, nor do they show your location in any manner whatsoever.

Inbound.—Cables and radiograms should be addressed to you, giving your full name, Army serial number, and *cable* address, but not your unit nor organization.

Talk

SILENCE MEANS SECURITY.—If violation of protective measures is serious within written communications it is disastrous in conversations. Protect your conversation as you do your letters, and be even more careful. A harmful letter can be nullified by censorship; loose talk is direct delivery to the enemy.

If you come home during war your lips must remain sealed and your writing hand must be guided by self-imposed censorship. This takes guts. Have you got them or do you want your buddies and your country to pay the price for your showing off? You've faced the battle front; it's little enough to ask you to face this "home front."

Capture

Most enemy intelligence comes from prisoners. If captured, you are required to give only three facts: YOUR NAME, YOUR GRADE, YOUR ARMY SERIAL NUMBER. Don't talk, don't try to fake stories, and use every effort to destroy all papers. When you are going into an area where capture is possible carry only essential papers and plan to destroy them prior to capture if possible. Do not carry personal letters on your person; they tell much about you, and the envelope has on it your unit and organization.

Be sensible; use your head

Published for the information and guidance of all concerned.
By order of the Secretary of War:

G. C. MARSHALL,
Chief of Staff.

Official:
J. A. ULIO,
Major General,
The Adjutant General.

U. S. GOVERNMENT PRINTING OFFICE: 1943

CAPTAIN HUBERT N. STURDIVANT AND COMMUNICATIONS SECTION - 2 -
8th AIR FORCE

ALCONBURY, ENGLAND   -   -   MAY 23, 1945

Above:
Capt Hubert Sturdivant and his men from the Communications Section at Alconbury, 1945. *J. Steininger/113 Association*

'Preparation for missions consisted of arising at 02.00hrs, breakfast of real eggs, ham, coffee and that thick crusted English bread. Mission briefing gave us the weather and assigned our Gee position over the English Channel which was relative to the other squadron aircraft. Also, the timing of our jammers, both on and off. Take-off was usually between 04.00 and 05.00hrs, in order to be in position ahead of the bomber formations that we would be screening, and which at that time would be forming over England. Visibility for most missions was so bad that aircraft awaiting take-off ahead of you were just about seen, and resulted in a number of accidents. One resulted in me becoming the possessor of an A-2 leather flying jacket, formerly owned by Glenwood

Poindexter, who was in a crew which reported at Cheddington with us.

'Usually four to eight aircraft would take-off thirty minutes before the bombers, to position singly about 10 miles apart, in an arc 50 miles east of the bomber assembly area. We would then fly a counter-clockwise racetrack orbit and jamming transmissions made for two to three hours as altitude was increased. Our screen would gradually advance towards the enemy territory or was shifted towards the North Sea. Whilst flying the racetrack, we occasionally observed the bright arc of a V-2 rocket vapour trail, lit by the rising sun as it ascended from the still dark horizon. These we could report, in the hope that action would and could be taken.

'As daylight appeared and we observed the bomber formations approaching from the west, we shut down our jamming equipment and dodged our way back to Cheddington, through the high, low and medium altitude squadrons, coasting out on their bombing missions.'

Loss of the Beast

February saw 24 VHF screening missions in support of the 8th AF and for the first time no aircraft provided a 'Mandrel' screen for the RAF. A total of 156 aircraft had been dispatched with the loss of just two. The first was on the 5th of the month when Liberator 42-51239 coded R4-C *Uninvited*, with a crew of 10, failed to return from its mission. All crew members were reported MIA — presumed shot down over the North Sea and drowned, as this was the area for their RCM patrol. On the 19th, *The Beast of*

Left:
I Walk Alone said it all for a 36th Bomb Squadron aircraft.
L. McCarthy/113 Association

Bourbon, painted with very colourful nose art in the form of a monster, crashed on take-off for a mission. This Liberator, 42-50385 R4-H, with a crew of 10, included two members of another crew. They were being taken on a 'check-out ride' to assess their capabilities for combat after completion of their squadron training. **Henry Parke**, who was a radio operator/gunner on Bert Young's crew, remembers that day:

'I flew most of my missions on Bert's crew, but then had a spell in hospital. When I came out my crew had completed their tour but I was left with 10 or so missions to do. Carl Boehm had lost his crew except for his co-pilot over the Irish Sea, because they were not wearing life jackets, so I talked him into taking a few of us "left-overs" as crew, to complete our tour. He agreed and we were known as "Boehm's Bums"! We were scheduled to fly on the 19th but were told another crew had one more mission to fly, so we let them have our ship to fly the mission. If we had not . . .'

The weather at Cheddington was poor, with visibility only 100yd in fog. With a wind speed of only 2mph from the south-southeast, there was little chance of an early clearing. In fact, by the time of take-off at 09.15hrs, the fog had closed visibility to 30yd! The

Liberator, with brakes released, rumbled out to the marshalling point next to runway 26. The captain, Louis McCarthy and Vic Pregeant, who was with him being checked out, made a pre-take-off check which showed everything to be in order. One last engine run-up was made, perhaps because the aircraft had been in dock for engine work the day before, but all was well. Brakes were released and, when the ground speed reached 105mph, rotation. The *Beast* took to the air and reached 110mph by the time the runway had been cleared. Due to the poor visibility, flying was immediately on instruments with the aircraft being held in a flying attitude to build up air speed to 135mph. All engines were operating at full throttle and sounding normal, with gauges indicating 43in of vacuum and 2,500rpm. Within half-a-mile of the runway, and just to the right, the *Beast* came down. The mark of its path indicated that it was in a proper attitude at the time of contact, and the altimeter showed 45ft — as it had not reduced. After hitting hedges and trees, Louis cut the throttles and Vic Pregeant cut the ignition switches, which possibly delayed the fire and explosion that took place within minutes of the crash. A local farmhand, seeing the tragic event, rushed over to help. Despite being burned, he removed three trapped members from the burning hulk. Three gunners, Pts Fred Becker and Howard Haley, and SSgt Carl Lindquist, were all killed.

Alconbury

February came to a black and very sad end for the squadron. It was not just the crashes that were responsible, tragic as they were, for on the 27th the whole squadron left Cheddington for a new base — the airfield at Alconbury in Cambridgeshire. This move was the beginning of the rundown for operations at Cheddington and, had the 36th remained, the airfield would have witnessed the activities that continued at Alconbury. These consisted of the continuation of 8th AF VHF screens and, from the 16th, actual jamming of enemy radar during the Bomb Group assembly period. In addition to these Liberator missions, there was the start of operations by three P-38J 'Droop Snoot' Lightning aircraft. These were flown by 7th Photographic Group pilots from Mount Farm, Oxfordshire, but used 36th Bomb Squadron observers — Lts Zeider, Holt and Stallcup — on the six ELINT missions which were flown. These were to monitor enemy radar in Holland and along the German front line. Of the three P-38s, one was reported MIA, and 43-28479 crashed on take-off. A take-off crash also caused the loss of Liberator 42-50844 on 20 March 1945 whilst being flown by Lt Sweeney, but this was thankfully the squadron's last Liberator accident and was non-fatal.

May 1945 gave way to new — but short-lived — missions in June, with the transportation of squadron members on 'sightseeing' trips over Germany. Ten passengers were carried at a time, with a minimum of crew to man the aircraft. Forty-four of

Below:
Alconbury — General arrangement.

these flights were flown during the month, plus 134 other 'passengers' to Paris for their 48hr pass. The only other flights made were celestial navigation night flights, for the benefit of the 20 squadron navigators preparing for the long flight back home to America. The order for these return flights came from 1st Air Division on 5 July 1945, and directed that the squadron's 20 Liberators, with Capt Jack Wrenn leading in 42-95221 *Ready N' Able*, depart via RAF Valley by the best available air route to Bradley Field, Windsor Locks, Connecticut, then on to Camp Miles Standish, Boston, for 'rest and recuperation'.

And so the electronic war against the Nazi regime was over, and with it the protection that crews in both the Mighty Eighth and Royal Air Force had been given by the 36th. This protection from the prying eyes and sharp ears of the enemy prevented, or hindered, them from bringing their guns to bear on the Allied bomber formations and fighter escorts. And that, without doubt, resulted in the saving of many, many Allied lives.

652ND BOMB SQUADRON (H)
ALCONBURY, ENGLAND — AUGUST 1945

Above:
R4-B with its underwing 'Mandrell' and 'Dina' antennae. On top of the fuselage is a 'Jostle' antenna.
M. Wrenn/113 Association

Above right:
A fine air-to-air shot of late-built B-24 45-0772 R4-B, taken from Jack's aircraft.
M. Wrenn/113 Association

Right:
Jack relaxes from the rigours of operational flying with a round of golf. *M. Wrenn/113 Association*

Right:
A view of Jack's B-24 cockpit showing the tail of B-24J 44-10609 R4-S.
M. Wrenn/113 Association

Far right:
Jack Wrenn with *Ready n' Able*.
M. Wrenn/113 Association

Below right:
The men of the 1077th Signal Company go 'State-side' on the *Queen Elizabeth*.
B. Downs/113 Association

Bottom:
The most photographed B-24 at Cheddington, *The Beast of Bourbon*, with Lt Jack Wrenn and his crew — 5 January 1945.
113 Association

VI
THE REUNION

The sky was blue with just an odd fluff of white cloud. A small group of men and women gathered in silence. Lost for words, their thoughts known only to themselves, they gazed skywards as a formation of aircraft approached. That group, which included a navigator, pilots and gunners from both Night Leaflet and RCM squadrons, aircraft mechanics, a communication expert and the captain of the Women's Army Corps along with some of her girls, could see 'Star and Bar' markings on the aircraft. There was no battle damage to be seen, or flares being fired to indicate injured or dead on board. As the formation made its third pass, a lone Piper Cub broke away, circled, then made a final run towards the group. When overhead, its pilot released a bundle of leaflets that fluttered to the ground. Not propaganda leaflets or news of the Allied armies' advance, but each one bearing the name of every man killed whilst based at Cheddington during World War 2. What the group had seen through their tears was not a formation of bombers overflying Cheddington during the war years, but a formation of nine light aircraft overflying Cheddington in the 1980s. This event marked the second reunion of the Cheddington

(STN 113) Association. The first was when a memorial was dedicated to the 8th AF on the site of Cheddington's old main gate.

Why had there been a reunion? Back in 1980 I tried to find out about the old airfield. Its buildings were empty, the runways gone. I searched books and official records — all to no avail. I decided that my only option open would be to form an Association with the aim of tracing as many as possible of those who had been based at Cheddington and obtain first-hand their experiences of those events and missions. Missions that until now had escaped attention, and had not been given the credit they deserved. Missions that were held in conditions of such secrecy that even some members of the aircraft crews did not know why, or where they were going! Those missions, and the assistance they received from the various support units, enabled many Allied lives to be saved, and tactics proven to such a degree that operations with the same structure are tasked to this day.

To all those who either supported or served with those 'Secret Squadrons', I say thank you.

AIR FORCE INTELLIGENCE SERVICE
UNITED STATES AIR FORCE

CERTIFICATE OF APPRECIATION
TO
The Cheddington (STN 113) ASSOCIATION

for the honor of participating
in the dedication of the
CHEDDINGTON MEMORIAL
as a representative of
THE UNITED STATES AIR FORCE

20 OCTOBER 1982

WALTER R. LONGANECKER, JR.
Major General, USAFR
Mobilization Assistant to the
Assistant Chief of Staff, Intelligence

Left:
Certificate of Appreciation.
**In 1980 the Cheddington
(STN 113) Association was
formed with the following aims:**

1. **To research past events at AAF Station 113, Cheddington**
2. **To locate those who served there with the US 8th AF**
3. **To erect a memorial to all those killed.**

Some 700 men and women have now been located. At the Association's first reunion in 1982 when a memorial was dedicated, Maj-Gen Walter Longanecker, USAFR, presented the Association with a Certificate of Appreciation from the Air Force Intelligence Service, USAF.

APPENDICES

Research Sources

United Kingdom
Imperial War Museum, London
Public Record Office, Kew
RAF Museum, London
Science Museum, London

United States of America
US Air Force Historical Research Center, Maxwell AFB, Alabama
Battle Monuments Commission, Washington DC, Defence Audio
    Visual Agency, Washington DC
US Air Force Inspection & Safety Center, Norton AFB, California

---

Selective Bibliography

8th Air Force Yearbook, J. Woolnough, (8AF News, Texas, 1981)
Air Force Spoken Here, J. Parton, (Adler, Maryland, 1986)
A Thousand Shall Fall, M. Peden, (Canada's Wings, Stittsville, 1981)
Carpetbaggers, B. Parnell, (Eakin Press, Texas, 1987)
Confound and Destroy, M. Streetly, (Macdonald & Jane's, London, 1978)
Fortress of the Big Triangle First, C. Bishop, (East Anglia, 1986)
Iron Eagle, T. Coffey, (Crown, New York, 1986)
Luftwaffe Handbook, A. Price, (Ian Allan, London, 1977)
Mighty Eighth, R. Freeman, (Macdonald & Jane's, London, 1970)
Mighty Eighth War Diary, R. Freeman, (Jane's, London, 1981)
Mighty Eighth War Manual, R. Freeman (Jane's, London, 1984)
Mission With LeMay, Gen C. LeMay, (Doubleday, New York, 1965)
US Strategic Bomber, R. Freeman, (Macdonald & Janes, London, 1975)

Unpublished Primary Source Material

Maxwell AFB, Alabama

B0797/8	2nd CCRC Group
A092	9th Station Complement Squadron
B0548/9	36th Service Group, USAAF
B0811	38th Service Group, USAAF
A0606/7	406th Bomb Squadron, USAAF
A0609	422nd Bomb Squadron, USAAF
A0667	858th Bomb Squadron, USAAF
A0464	1077th Signal Company, USAAF
B5118	Composite Command Records
A0470	Station 113 Records

Public Record Office, Kew

AIR	14/737	RCM Equipment
AIR	14/1427	Operation 'Infatuate'
AIR	14/6005	Leaflet Policy
AIR	20/1492	RCM 1939-45
AIR	25/777	No 100 Group Operations
AIR	28/104	RAF Bovingdon Operations Record Book (ORB)
AIR	28/143	RAF Cheddington ORB
AIR	29/669	RAF Wing ORB

Aircraft Used by 406th Bomb Squadron (NL)

SERIAL	TYPE	CODE	NAME/COMMENTS
42-38167	B-17G	JJ-L	—
42-6174	B-17F	JJ-K	Home-Sick Angel/Stripped for Action
43-37516	B-17G	JJ-T	Tondalayo. Shot down Clacton 4/3/45
530	B-17		W/O 10/7/44
43-37530	B-17G	JJ-A	W/O 4/1/45
42-30656	B-17F	JJ-D	Miss Mickey Finn, also JJ-W
42-37717	B-17G	JJ-B	Channel Fever Baby
42-37726	B-17G	JJ-N	Shady Lady
42-37771	B-17G	JJ-Q	—
42-30775	B-17G	JJ-P	—
42-39790	B-17G	JJ-F	—
42-30791	B-17F	JJ-J	Pistol Packin' Mama
42-59811	B-17G	JJ-E	MIA 6/7/44
42-30838	B-17F	JJ-0	Paper Doll
42-39843	B-17G	JJ-G	Daley's Male
42-51210	B-24H	J6-0	—
42-51217	B-24H	J6-R	—
42-37522	B-24H	J6-	Miss Stardust
42-95238	B-24H	J6-K	W/O 18/8/44
42-52251	B-24J	J6-L	—
42-50479	B-24J	J6-L	—
42-50483	B-24J	J6-I	Midnite Mistress
42-50484	B-24J	J6-	W/O 21/1/45
42-51492	B-24J	J6-B	—
42-52510	B-24J	J6-U	—
41-29522	B-24H		856BS on DS. W/O 11/12/44
42-50555	B-24J	J6-G	—
42-51555	B-24J	J6-Q	—
41-29602	B-24H		856BS on DS
42-51574	B-24J	J6-P	—
41-29598	B-24H		—
41-29599	B-24H	J6-	—
41-29601	B-24H	J6-M	—
41-29602	B-24H	J6-Q	856BS on DS. Black Zombie
44-10619	B-24J	J6-T	—
42-52637	B-24H		—
42-52650	B-24H	J6-E	W/O 3/1/45
42-50651	B-24J	J6-F	—
42-50652	B-24J	J6-W	Dark Eyes
42-94756	B-24H	J6-C	—
42-94775	B-24H	J6-	W/O 18/11/44
42-94824	B-24H	J6-S	—
42-39845	B-24H	J6-	W/O 12/10/44
42-94851	B-24H	J6-E	—
42-94865	B-24H	J6-H	—
869	B-24H	J6-	—
41-28871	B-24H	J6-	The Leading Lady. Crashed 14/3/45
42-94873	B-24H	J6-Y	—
41-28880	B-24H	J6-Y	—
44-50929	B-24M	J6-	—
42-50844	B-24J	J6-	—
41-6205	P-47C		—

Named aircraft that are unknown

—	—	—	Swing Shift
—	—	—	Foxy Lady
—	—	—	She Wolf
—	B-24H	J6-	The Night Night
—	—	—	Betty

(W/O = Written Off; DS = Detached Service; MIA = Missing in Action)

422/858/406th Bomb Squadron
Mission Summary

CHELVESTON: October 1943-June 1944
Missions: 128
Sorties: 662
Leaflets: 536,220,000 (6,703 bundles)

CHEDDINGTON: 27 June 1944-13 March 1945
Missions: 160
Sorties: 1,292
Leaflets: 1,121,600,000
L/Bombs: 14,020

HARRINGTON: 14 March 1945-25 April 1945
Missions: 27
Sorties: 378
Leaflets: 285,580,000
L/Bombs: 3,571

TOTAL: October 1943-25 April 1945
Missions: 315
Sorties: 2,332
Leaflets: 1,943,500,000
L/Bombs: 24,294
Targets: 6,816
Pigeons: 200

6 June 1944 — D-Day
Missions: 1
Sorties: 6
Leaflets: 3,000,000
L/Bombs: 60

Tons of leaflets dropped by all 8th Air Force Units
October 1943-May 1945

MONTH	UNITS ON BOMBING MISSIONS	422/406th BOMB SQN	492nd BOMB GRP	MONTHLY TOTALS
1943				
Oct	—	24.4	—	24.4
Nov	—	100.8	—	100.8
Dec	3.3	112.1	—	115.4
1944				
Jan	27.6	118.6	3.8	150.0
Feb	37.4	131.6	6.9	175.9
Mar	99.1	146.3	12.9	258.3
Apr	74.8	134.9	27.9	237.6
May	123.5	102.4	35.3	261.2
Jun	73.1	209.6	43.1	325.8
Jul	53.6	216.1	42.3	312.0
Aug	87.8	203.1	37.6	328.5
Sep	152.8	180.4	1.1	334.3
Oct	165.8	240.5	—	406.3
Nov	151.1	315.3	—	466.4
Dec	138.1	261.6	—	399.7
1945				
Jan	165.8	182.0	—	347.8
Feb	196.6	276.3	—	472.9
Mar	247.0	407.9	—	654.9
Apr	186.8	370.5	—	557.3
May	102.4	—	—	102.4
	2,086.6	3,734.4	210.9	6,031.9

In May 1945, the 406th Bomb Squadron flew four missions of 30 sorties over 56 targets. 354 leaflet bombs were dropped containing 28,320,000 leaflets. After VE-Day, 18 non-combat missions of 141 sorties over 96 targets were flown. 1,549 bombs were used.

Aircraft Used by 36th Bomb Squadron (RCM)

SERIAL	TYPE	CODE	NAME/COMMENTS
42-3438	B-17F	—	—
42-3518	B-17G	—	—
42-6080	B-17F	—	—
42-30039	B-17F	—	Liberty Belle
42-30066	B-17F	—	—
42-30114	B-17F	—	—
42-30177	B-17F	—	—
42-30178	B-17F	—	—
42-30353	B-17F	—	—
42-30363	B-17F	—	—
42-37743	B-17G	—	—
41-29144	B-24	R4-B	—
42-51188	B-24H	R4-O	Lady Jane. First 'Dina'-equipped aircraft
42-51219	B-24H	R4-I	W/O 15/11/44
42-95221	B-24H	R4-A	Margie/Ready N'Able
42-51226	B-24J	R4-L	W/O 10/11/44
42-51230	B-24J	R4-E	Li'l Pudge/Rum Dum
42-51232	B-24J	R4-J	W/O 22/12/44
42-51239	B-24J	R4-C	Uninvited. MIA North Sea 5/2/45
42-51304	B-24J	R4-B	—
42-51307	B-24J	R4-Q	—
42-51308	B-24J	R4-M	Modest Maid
42-51311	B-24J	R4-T	—
42-51315	B-24J	R4-U	—
42-50385	B-24H	R4-H	Beast of Bourbon. W/O 19/2/45
42-50476	B-24J	R4-J	—
42-50495	B-24J	R4-V	—
44-50502	B-24	R4-C	—
44-10507	B-24J	R4-	—
42-95507	B-24J	R4-D	Maintenance only. RCM School
42-51546	B-24J	R4-L	I Walk Alone
42-50576	B-24	R4-H	—
41-29593	B-24	R4-	—
42-7607	B-24H	R4-A	—
44-10609	B-24J	R4-S	—
42-50622	B-24J	R4-N	This is it Men/Bama Bound-Lovely Libba
42-50665	B-24J	R4-K	Lady in The Dark
42-50671	B-24J	R4-F	Ramp Rooster
42-51685	B-24J	R4-R	Playmate
42-50750	B-24J	R4-P	—
42-40796	B-24	R4-	—
42-94811	B-24J	R4-I	Miss-B-Haven
44-23156	P-38	R4-	—
43-28479	P-38	R4-	Crashed 25/6/45
44-23501	P-38	R4-	—
44-23515	P-38	R4-	MIA

Named aircraft that are unknown

	TYPE	CODE	NAME/COMMENTS
—	B-24	R4-	Black Magic
—	B-24	R4-	The Jigs Up
—	B-24	R4-	The Gypsy Jane

36th Bomb Squadron

Missions

6 June 1944-30 April 1945

JUNE 1944

Date	Sorties
5/6	4
16/17	6
17/18	5
22/23	6
27/28	5
28/29	5

JULY 1944

Date	Sorties
4/5	5
7/8	5
9/10	5
12/13	5
14/15	5
17/18	4
19/20	4
20/21	4
21/22	3
23/24	5
24/25	3
25/26	3
28/29	4
29/30	3

AUGUST 1944

Date	Sorties
4/5	2
6/7	5
7/8	5
8/9	5
9/10	4
10/11	4
11/12	4
12/13	5
13/14	4
16/17	4
17/18	2
18/19	6
25/26	6
26/27	7
27/28	6
29/30	4
30/31	6

SEPTEMBER 1944

Date	Sorties
1/2	4
5/6	4
6/7	4
8/9	4
9/10	4
10/11	3
11/12	5
12/13	6
13/14	6
15/16	7
16/17	5
17/18	6
18/19	7
22/23	4
23/24	6
25/26	3
26/27	4
28/29	5

OCTOBER 1944

Date	Sorties
5/6	5
6/7	7
7/8	6
9/10	7
14/15	7
15/16	6
19/18	7
21/22	8
23/24	6
24/25	6
26/27	6
30/31	7
31/1	7

NOVEMBER 1944

Date	Sorties
1/2	7
2/3	7
4/5	5
6/7	8
9/9	7
10/11	8
11/12	7
15/16	5
18/19	6
20/21	5
21/22	6
23/24	6
25	6
25/26	3
26	8
26/27	3
27	5
27/28	3
28	8
28/29	2
29	7
29/30	2
30	6
30/31	2

DECEMBER 1944

Date	Sorties
1	7
1/2	1
2	6
2/3	2
3	7
4	8
4/5	2
5	9
6	8
6/7	2
7	8
8	10
9	10
9/10	1
10	8
11	9
12	8
12/13	1
13	3
15	6
16	5
17/18	1
18	9
18/19	1
19	8
23	2
24	5
25	8
28	9
30	5
30/31	1
31	7

JANUARY 1945

Date	Sorties
1/2	1
2	7
2/3	1
3	4
5	10
6	5
7	7
8	6
9	5
10	4
13	6
15	6
16	5
17	7
18	7
20	8
21	6
23	5
24	6
26	3
28	5
29	5
31	7

FEBRUARY 1945

Date	Sorties
1	7
2	6
3	7
5	9
6	8
7	6
8	6
9	6
10	6
11	6
14	7
15	7
16	7
17	6
19	2
20	7
21	7
22	7
23	7
24	7
25	7
26	6
27	6
28	6

MARCH 1945

Date	Sorties
1	6
2	5
3	4
5	2
6	2
7	5
8	5
9	4
10	5
11	5
12	5
14	5
15	5
16	13
17	14
18	13
19	15
20	11
21	11
22	4
23	12
24	9
24	3
25	5
26	4
27	14
30	13
31	3

APRIL 1945

Date	Sorties
2	4
3	5
3	4
4	4
5	4
6	5
7	4
8	4
10	4
11	4
12	4
13	5
16	4
17	4
18	4
19	4
20	4
23	4
25	3

36th Bomb Squadron
Mission Summary

5 June 1944-30 April 1945

TYPE OF OPERATION	MISSIONS	FROM/TO
RAF Radar Screen	97	5/6/44-3/1/45
VHF Screen	122	25/11/44-30/4/45
'Spoof'	3	28/11/44-8/12/44
'Jackal'	5	28/12/44-7/1/45
AAF Radar Screen	10	16/3/44-30/3/45
B-24 Search	16	7/3/45-3/4/45
P-38 Search	8	17/3/45-13/4/45

June 1944		*July 1944*	
Total Missions	6	Total Missions	19
Total Sorties	31	Total Sorties	58
Aborts	3	Aborts	4

August 1944		*September 1944*	
Total Missions	17	Total Missions	18
Total Sorties	79	Total Sorties	87
Aborts	6	Aborts	1

October 1944		*November 1944*	
Total Missions	13	Total Missions	24
Total Sorties	85	Total Sorties	131
Aborts	4	Aborts	4

December 1944		*January 1945*	
Total Missions	32	Total Missions	24
Total Sorties	177	Total Sorties	133
Aborts	8	Aborts	8

February 1945		*March 1945*	
Total Missions	24	Total Missions	28
Total Sorties	156	Total Sorties	202
Aborts	1	Aborts	5

April 1945	
Total Missions	20
Total Sorties	78
Aborts	2

36th Bomb Squadron (RCM)
Letter of Commendation

14 November 1944
TO:
Commanding Officer, AAF Station 113, US Army,
(Attention: Commanding Officer, 36th Bomb Squadron)

1. This Headquarters has received a confidential message D-67417, dated 13 November 1944, from the Commanding General of the Eighth Air Force. This message is quoted below.

'Attention Commanding Officer 36th Bomb Squadron RCM. Jamming, screening, and diversionary efforts of the 36th Bomb Squadron have contributed greatly to the effects of the RAF bombing efforts. Mission of 9/10 November was one of the most effective in confusing the GAF and causing them to assemble in great haste to intercept the bomb stream which was not there, and reflects great credit to the Command and the individuals concerned. Signed Doolittle.'

2. This Command forwards this message from General Doolittle with great pleasure and wishes to add its own commendation for a job extremely well done.

By order of Colonel Webster

(Signed)
Richard N. Ellis,
Lt-Colonel, Air Corps,
Chief of Staff

36th Bomb Squadron (RCM)
Letter of Commendation

23 May 1945
TO:
Commanding Officer, 36th Bomb Squadron (RCM), APO 557,
(Thru: Commanding General, 1st Air Div)

1. The advance of the Allied Ground Forces has exposed the effectiveness of air bombardment activities in the destruction of the fighting potentialities of our enemy. The special operations conducted by the 36th Bombardment Squadron (RCM) cannot be over-emphasized in the contribution of the unit to the striking power of this Air Force.

2. Each individual in the organization expended great effort in extensive training in new equipment which you used operationally for the first time on the night of 5th/6th June 1944. Cooperating with the RAF, they provided an efficient radar screen of the enemy early warning system. Individual activities of every member of your Command combined to effect the greatest possible chance of total success not only for this operation but for all operations to follow.

3. The organization, throughout its relatively short but colourful history, has displayed the highest type of initiative and performance. Lacking the glory of combat over enemy territory, your missions were still carried on under the most hazardous of weather conditions. At times, you were still successfully carrying out your missions when it was necessary to issue orders standing down all combat operations.

4. Yours was the assignment of catching the enemy at his own game, and in effectively accomplishing this task, the whole nature and tactics of your missions changed as the enemy scientists devise methods of overcoming our counter-measures. The complexity of your work included jamming of enemy radar, screening of our bomber VHF channels while bombers were assembling, carrying out 'spoof' raids, jamming enemy tank communications, and performing special electronic search missions as directed by this Headquarters. The material advantage of these operations may never be adequately assessed and it is impossible to fully evaluate the number of air crews, as well as bomber and fighter aircraft, saved when enemy fighters discovered too late the essential interception data.

5. Hardwork, exceptional technical ability and determination to see a job well done enabled the 36th Bomb Squadron (RCM) to successfully carry out this mission and reflected high credit upon the whole Eighth Air Force.

6. It is my desire that this commendation be disseminated to all members of your Command.

(Signed) W. E. Kepner,
Major-General, US Army,
Commanding.

Other Known Unit Aircraft

SERIAL	TYPE	CODE	UNIT/COMMENTS
8th Weather Flight			
42-39871	B-17G	'H'	Crashed St Eval
42-37869	B-17G		Crashed Okehampton
39th Service Group			
43-7482	Cessna UC-78		Bobcat (transport variant)
44-70393	Noorduyn C-64A Norseman		
43-14485	Fairchild UC-61		Forwarder
42-58189	Cessna AT-17 Bobcat		Burnt out Cheddington 31/8/44
	(training variant)		
495th Fighter Training Group			
44-70292	Noorduyn C-64A Norseman		
Courier Squadron			
42-98996	Vultee L-5		
42-98997	Vultee L-5		
42-78998	Vultee L-5		
12/2/4 CRCC			
41-24500	B-17F		Ex-381BG. *Annie Freeze*
42-40801	B-24D		
11 CCRC			
41-2578	B-17E		Ex-97BG. *Butcher Shop.* On first AF mission
41-2628	B-17E		Ex-97BG
41-9013	B-17E		Ex-97BG
41-9021	B-17E		Ex-97BG. *Hangar Queen.* First 8AF mid-air collision
41-9025	B-17E		Ex-97BG. *Little John*
41-9089	B-17E		Ex-97BG. *Johny Reb.* First 8AF fatal
41-9100	B-17E		Ex-97BG. *Birmingham Blitzkreig*
41-9119	B-17E		Ex-97BG
41-9121	B-17E		Ex-97BG. *The Big Bitch*
41-9174	B-17E		Ex-97BG

Composite Command

Airfields

NUMBER	NAME	OPERATIONS
102	Alconbury	Pathfinder
112	Bovingdon	B-17 CCRC
113	Cheddington	B-24 CCRC, Leaflet, RCM, AFCC HQ
172	Snettisham	B-17 Gunnery School
179	Harrington	'Carpetbagger', Leaflet
236	Toome	A-20 CCRC, B-26 CCRC
237	Greencastle	B-24/Anti-Aircraft Gunnery School
238	Cluntoe	B-24 CCRC
342	Atcham	P-47 CCRC, P-38 CCRC
345	Goxhill	P-51 CCRC

Airfield Staffing Levels — August 1944

AAF STN	COMPOSITE COMMAND Off	COMPOSITE COMMAND EM	OTHER COMMANDS Off	OTHER COMMANDS EM	STUDENTS TRAINING Off	STUDENTS TRAINING EM	TOTAL STAFF Off	TOTAL STAFF EM
102	339	1,850	5	234	75	177	419	2,261
112	152	1,257	37	193	579	—	768	1,450
113	371	2,031	25	209	—	—	396	2,240
172	42	585	4	24	—	781	46	1,390
179	461	213	1	4	—	—	462	217
236	110	1,231	1	11	329	333	440	1,575
237	63	1,019	—	—	13	724	76	1,743
238	177	1,072	1	11	335	87	513	1,170
342	132	1,220	2	16	353	—	487	1,236
345	123	1,353	2	20	445	—	570	1,373
TOTAL	1,970	11,831	78	722	2,129	2,102	4,177	14,655

(Note: *Off* = Officers; *EM* = Enlisted Men.)

Unit Staffing Levels — August 1944

UNIT ASSIGNED	AAF STN	TOTAL STAFF
Headquarters & Headquarters Squadron Composite Command	416	416
Headquarters & Headquarters Squadron CCRC Group	451	1,804
Replacement & Training Squadron	303	1,214
Headquarters & Headquarters Squadron Fighter Training Group	224	448
Fighter Training Squadron	603	1,207
Bomb Group Headquarters	178	357
Bomb Squadron	1,480	4,442
Air Division Gunnery School	518	518
Headquarters & Headquarters Squadron Service Group	120	482
Service Squadron	199	1,194
Station Complement Squadron	124	1,120
Military Police Company	85	852
Signal Company	54	491
Ordnance Supply & Maintenance Company	62	564
Quartermaster Company	40	359
Gunnery & Tow Target Flight	23	117
Engineering Fire Fighting Platoon	15	117
Medical Dispensary	19	39
Finance Detachment	12	224
Weather Detachment		

(This table shows the average number of personnel attached to each unit of Composite Command on an airfield, and also the total personnel in the Command.)

Consolidated Aircraft Report — August 1944

TYPE	B-17	B-24	B-26	P-38	P-47	P-51	A-20	Other	TOTAL
On hand	79	94	26	18	71	40	5	63	396
Serviceable	61	71	19	15	57	29	3	48	303
Grounded	18	23	7	3	14	11	2	15	93
GROUNDED									
General maintenance	13	19	5	3	14	9	1	8	72
Parts	2	2	2	0	0	2	1	7	16
Other	3	2	0	0	0	0	0	0	5
% ON HAND									
Serviceable	77	76	73	83	80	73	60	76	77
Grounded	23	24	27	17	20	27	40	24	23
General maintenance	16	20	19	17	20	22	20	13	18
Parts	3	2	8	0	0	5	20	11	18
Other	4	2	0	0	0	0	0	0	1
FLYING HOURS									
Ops	569	3,312	—	—	—	—	—	84	3,965
Non-Ops	3,319	1,374	833	553	7,365	3,951	86	1,443	18,924
Total	3,888	4,686	833	553	7,365	3,951	86	1,527	22,889
AVERAGE	49.1	49.5	32.1	30.4	103.4	98.5	17.1	24.1	57.5

Aircraft Use — August 1944

AAF STATION NUMBER HQ	102	112	113	172	179	236	237	238	342	345	TOTAL
On Hand											
10	49	18	16	14	6	64	35	12	32	8	56	320
Serviceable											
7	39	13	10	12	4	52	28	9	18	68	43	303
Grounded											
3	10	5	6	2	22	12	7	34	14	16	13	144
GROUNDED											
General maintenance											
3	8	2	6	2	1	9	5	1	11	16	11	75
For parts											
0	2	2	0	0	1	1	2	2	3	0	2	15
Other											
0	3	0	0	0	0	2	0	0	0	0	0	5

AAF STATION NUMBER

	HQ	102	112	113	113	172	179	236	237	238	342	345	TOTAL
% ON HAND													
Serviceable	70	80	72	62	86	66	91	80	75	56	81	77	77
% GROUNDED													
General maintenance	30	20	11	38	14	17	14	14	9	34	19	20	18
For parts	0	4	17	0	0	17	2	6	16	10	0	3	4
Other	0	6	0	0	0	0	3	0	0	0	0	0	1
FLYING HOURS													
Operational	—	107	—	500	279	—	3,086	—	—	—	—	—	3,972
Non ops	340	2,755	439	32	117	266	905	1,123	192	702	7,358	4,695	18,924
TOTAL	340	2,862	439	532	386	266	3,991	1,123	192	702	7,358	4,695	22,896

Aircraft Allocation — August 1944

AIRCRAFT TYPE	HQ	102	112	113	172	179	236	237	238	342	345	TOTAL
B-17	1	45	12	13				2	7			80
B-24		1	2	21	2					16		42
B-26							25					25
P-38										18		18
P-39			1									1
P-47	1	1	1							68		71
P-51											4	4
A-20								1				1
Havoc								1				1
RB 25			1									1
L-4B			1				1	1	1	1	1	6
Oxford	3		1		1					1		6
UC-61A	2	1	1		1							5
UC-64A			1									1
UC-78A	1									1		2
C-47								4				4
AT-6										3	1	4
AT-16	1									2		3
AT-23	1						9					10
RA-35	1			5					8	6		20
YC-108			1									1
TOTAL	11	49	21	34	5	8	35	13	30	91	9	306

Total aircraft on hand with Composite Command August 1944

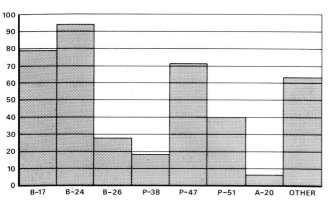

Aircraft Accident Summary — August 1944

TYPE	P-47	P-38	P-51	B-26	B-24	B-17	OTHER	TOTAL
TOTAL	17	6	19	3	3	0	6	54
FATAL	3	0	3	0	1	0	1	8
CAUSE								
Technique	10	3	11	1	0	0	2	27
Judgement	1	1	2	0	0	0	1	5
Careless	1	1	0	0	0	0	0	2
3rd Party	2	0	2	1	0	0	0	5
Airframe	3	1	3	1	2	0	2	12
Unknown	0	0	1	0	1	0	1	3
TOTAL	17	6	19	3	3	0	6	54
OCCURRED								
Taxying	1	1	4	0	0	0	1	7
Take-off	1	0	1	1	0	0	0	3
Flight	12	1	4	2	2	0	2	23
Landing	2	3	9	0	1	0	1	16
Emergency	1	1	1	0	0	0	2	5
TOTAL	17	6	19	3	3	0	6	54
DAMAGE								
Minor	0	0	0	1	0	0	0	1
Major	6	2	13	1	1	0	4	27
Wreck	8	4	6	1	2	0	2	23
TOTAL	14	6	19	3	3	0	6	51

CCRC Training — 1944

	MARCH	APRIL	MAY	JUNE	JULY	AUGUST
Graduated AAF STN 112 (B-17)	251	351	353	475	398	422
By-Passed CCRC	63	213	84	77	268	64
Arrived Stone Depot	315	544	579	417	680	486
Overall Attrition	353	350	372	285	296	364
Graduated AAF STN 236 (B-26)	28	97	62	69	62	116
Arrived Stone Depot	255	75	53	127	131	102
Graduated AAF STN 236 (A-20)	11	11	43	60	20	42
Arrived Stone Depot	11	45	103	35	65	33
Graduated AAF STN 238 (B-24)	49	116	224	328	382	315
By-Passed CCRC	27	—	92	10	12	19
Arrived Stone Depot	156	149	320	427	382	283
Overall Attrition	160	177	160	210	282	308
Graduated AAF STN 342 (P-47)	15	330	275	610	247	310
Arrived Stone Depot	141	487	494	250	342	328
Overall Attrition	92	99	124	131	209	86
Graduated AAF STN 342 (P-38)	51	99	156	144	114	51
Arrived Stone Depot	107	158	145	116	56	84
Overall Attrition	35	47	67	220	71	13
Graduated AAF STN 345 (P-51)	70	152	89	212	241	212
Arrived Stone Depot	80	190	192	108	340	451
Overall Attrition	100	129	134	168	99	220

Miscellaneous Training — 1944

STN	TRAINING SCHOOL	MARCH	APRIL	MAY	JUNE	JULY	AUGUST
237	Anti-Aircraft Gunnery School	689	843	868	862	480	287
237	B-24 Gunnery School	—	—	1,075	1,631	1,947	1,657
172	B-17 Gunnery School	1,528	1,146	2,169	2,432	2,031	2,929
102	Pathfinder Navigator School	39	65	75	66	80	74
113	Radar School	44	39	42	87	76	20
113	Personnel Equipment School	—	—	119	105	173	120

(Note: B-17/B-24 Gunnery Schools operated as an annexe to Stations 112 and 238.)

IN MEMORY

Interments at Cambridge Cemetery

RANK	NAME	UNIT	CAUSE OF DEATH
LCol	Earle Aber	406BS	*Hit by Allied anti-aircraft fire*
2Lt	Gilman Blake	406BS	*Struck aircraft after bailing out*
SSgt	Albany Blanchard	8AF WX	*Hit hill in Devon*
Sgt	Leslie Cazzell	856BS	*Crashed Oulton*
FO	Gerben Coehoorn	406BS	*Crashed Harrington*
2Lt	Maurice Harper	406BS	*Hit by Allied anti-aircraft fire*
2Lt	Cressy Kingery	406BS	*Crashed Madley*
2Lt	Walter Lamson	36BS	*Take-off crash*
Cpl	Dale Patterson	406BS	*Crashed Madley*
2Lt	Jarome Pfullman	406BS	*Take-off crash*
TSgt	Sherwood Renner	8AF WX	*Hit hill in Devon*
Sgt	William Repp	406BS	*Take-off crash*
Cpl	Maurice Rushing	406BS	*Crashed Madley*
PFC	Leonard Smith	36BS	*Take-off crash*
Cpl	Clarence Spect	406BS	*Crashed Madley*
Maj	Seymore Winslow	8AFCC	*Took own life with pistol*

Missing in Action

RANK	NAME	UNIT	CAUSE OF DEATH
Sgt	Robert Brass	36BS	*MIA North Sea*
SSgt	Ray Brecht	36BS	*MIA North Sea*
SSgt	Galen Brooke	36BS	*MIA North Sea*
SSgt	Arthur Clemens	36BS	*MIA Irish Sea*
Sgt	Charles Dautel	36BS	*MIA Irish Sea*
Sgt	Harold Eckert	36BS	*MIA North Sea*
SSgt	Jamie Forseca	36BS	*MIA Irish Sea*
Sgt	Paul Frantz	36BS	*MIA North Sea*
TS	Roger Gagne	36BS	*MIA Irish Sea*
Sgt	Bruce Gist	36BS	*MIA North Sea*
2Lt	Eugene Junkin	36BS	*MIA North Sea*
2Lt	William Lehner	36BS	*MIA Irish Sea*
SSgt	Francis Lynch	36BS	*MIA Irish Sea*
2Lt	John McKibben	36BS	*MIA North Sea*
2Lt	Gaylord Moulton	36BS	*MIA North Sea*
SSgt	Harvey Nystrom	36BS	*MIA Irish Sea*
SSgt	Andrew Zapotochy	36BS	*MIA North Sea*
Sgt	Max Oeitle	36BS	*MIA North Sea*

Interments Elsewhere

RANK	NAME	UNIT	CAUSE OF DEATH
2Lt	Gene Anderson	406BS	*Take-off crash*
Pte	Fred Becker	36BS	*Take-off crash*
1Lt	Fred Bofink	856BS	*Crashed Oulton*
1Lt	Chester Cherrington	406BS	*Crashed Madley on cross-country*
Sgt	William Daugherty	CCRC	*Bomb explosion Cheddington*
TSgt	Gordon Elmore	856BS	*Crashed Oulton*
2Lt	William Ferguson	406BS	*Hit by flak in France*
Cpl	Elmer Frieder	406BS	*Crashed Madley*
2Lt	Fred Gray	36BS	*Hit by flak in France*
Pte	Fred Haley	36BS	*Take-off crash*
SSgt	George Hawkes	406BS	*Take-off crash*
2Lt	Ray Hendrix	406BS	*Take-off crash*
2Lt	Walter Lawson	36BS	*Take-off crash*
1Lt	Fred Lemke	856BS	*Crashed Oulton*
SSgt	Carl Lindquest	36BS	*Take-off crash*
Sgt	Ray Mears	36BS	*Hit by flak in France*
2Lt	Charles Miller	406BS	*Take-off crash*
2Lt	Vincent Murphy	406BS	*Take-off crash*
2Lt	Richard Neary	8AF WX	*Hit hill in Devon*
SSgt	Marcia Panteei	8AF WX	*Hit hill in Devon*
SSgt	Garrett Parnell	856BS	*Crashed Oulton*
2Lt	Robert Preston	406BS	*Crashed Madley*
Sgt	Frank Bartho	36BS	*Hit by flak in France*
Cpl	Doug Reseigh	406BS	*Crashed Madley*
1Lt	James Rush	406BS	*Take-off crash*
Sgt	Sam Schaffer	406BS	*Take-off crash*
1Lt	Louis Sherman	CCRC	*Bomb explosion Cheddington*
Sgt	Blyth Smyth	406BS	*Take-off crash*
Sgt	Edmond Szymczak	406BS	*KIA oxygen loss*
Cpl	Robert Waite	406BS	*Crashed Madley*
Sgt	Josef Weik	406BS	*Take-off crash*
Sgt	John Wheatley	406BS	*Take-off crash*
2Lt	Donald Wilson	406BS	*Crashed Madley*
2Lt	Herman Wolters	36BS	*Electrical fault Belgium*

We Will Remember Them